Energy Conservation and Economic Growth

AAAS Selected Symposia Series

Energy Conservation and Economic Growth

Edited by Charles J. Hitch

NEW YORK AND LONDON

AAAS Selected Symposium **22**

First published 1978 by Westview Press, Inc.

Published 2021 by Routledge
605 Third Avenue, New York, NY 10017
2 Park Square, Milton Park, Abingdon, Oxon OX14 4RN

Routledge is an imprint of the Taylor & Francis Group, an informa business

Copyright © 1978 by the American Association for the
Advancement of Science

All rights reserved. No part of this book may be reprinted or reproduced or utilised in any
form or by any electronic, mechanical, or other means, now known or hereafter invented,
including photocopying and recording, or in any information storage or retrieval system,
without permission in writing from the publishers.

Notice:
Product or corporate names may be trademarks or registered trademarks, and are used
only for identification and explanation without intent to infringe.

Library of Congress Catalog Card Number: 78-66339
ISBN: 0-89158-354-8

ISBN 13: 978-0-3670-1817-7 (hbk)
ISBN 13: 978-0-3671-6804-9 (pbk)

DOI: 10.4324/9780429048036

About the Book

This volume goes to the heart of the continuing debate on national energy policy: to adjust to the expected higher cost of energy, how much should we rely on conserving energy and how much on increasing energy supplies? The special focus of the book is the impact of energy conservation on economic growth. Is it positive, negative, or neutral?

The authors agree that higher energy costs in themselves will have some dampening effect on growth. But can conservation mitigate this effect? If so, what kind and amount of conservation is needed, and how can it be achieved? The book's optimists see in energy constraints an opportunity to achieve simpler, cleaner lifestyles via conservation and to resuscitate a stagnant, underemployed economy by investment in conservation and supply technologies. Even the pessimistic contributors assign some role to conservation, albeit a limited one. They stress, however, the need for increasing energy supplies to fuel the economic growth they consider necessary to achieve many other national and international objectives. The skeptics (and all the authors are to some degree skeptical) call for more research, and some describe in detail what research is needed. The book's distinguishing characteristics are its balanced presentation of a variety of possible economic responses to higher energy costs and--though it is addressed to economists and policymakers--its accessibility to nonprofessional audiences.

About the Series

The *AAAS Selected Symposia Series* was begun in 1977 to provide a means for more permanently recording and more widely disseminating some of the valuable material which is discussed at the AAAS Annual National Meetings. The volumes in this *Series* are based on symposia held at the Meetings which address topics of current and continuing significance, both within and among the sciences, and in the areas in which science and technology impact on public policy. The *Series* format is designed to provide for rapid dissemination of information, so the papers are not typeset but are reproduced directly from the camera-copy submitted by the authors, without copy editing. The papers are organized and edited by the symposium arrangers who then become the editors of the various volumes. Most papers published in this *Series* are original contributions which have not been previously published, although in some cases additional papers from other sources have been added by an editor to provide a more comprehensive view of a particular topic. Symposia may be reports of new research or reviews of established work, particularly work of an interdisciplinary nature, since the AAAS Annual Meetings typically embrace the full range of the sciences and their societal implications.

WILLIAM D. CAREY
Executive Officer
American Association for
the Advancement of Science

Contents

List of Figures	ix
List of Tables and Charts	xiii
About the Editor and Authors	xv
Introduction-- *Charles J. Hitch*	1
1 The Imperative of Energy Conservation for Economic Growth--*John H. Gibbons*	5
2 The Consistency of Economic Growth and Energy Conservation Technology-- *Chauncey Starr*	29

Introduction	29
Planning Target	31
International Energy Comparisons and Conservation Potential	33
New Technology Integration	36
Planning Philosophy	39
Economic Growth and the Quality of Life	39
Economic Growth and Technology	41
Energy Conservation Technology	49
Energy Availability	51
Conclusions	55
References	56

3 Energy and Full Employment--*W.W. Rostow*	59

A Prima Facie Argument	59
The Effects of a Rise in Relative Price of a Major Basic Commodity: A Few Historical Illustrations	62

vii

viii *Table of Contents*

Energy-Economy Models and the Energy Problem of the United States	70
Required Energy Investment and the Return to Full Employment	79
Energy Investment: The Impact on the Regions	95
Conclusions	110

4 Lessons of History and Other Countries-- *Joel Darmstadter*   113

5 Post-Petroleum Prosperity-- *Denis Hayes*   125

6 The Fable of the Elephant and the Rabbit? -- *Alan S. Manne*   139

Energy-Economy Interactions	139
The Elephant and the Rabbit?	140
Empirical Evidence on Elasticities	145
Concluding Comments	150
References	151

7 Adjusting Capital Stock to Higher Energy-Using Efficiencies-- *Roger W. Sant*   153

Background	153
A General Approach to the Energy Demand Forecast Problem	158
The Residential Sector	158
The Industrial Sector	159
The Commercial Building and Transportation Sectors	161
The Integrating Tool	161
Preliminary Results	163
Conclusion	166
References	166

List of Figures

Chapter 1

Figure 1   Reduction in demand for scarce energy resources   6

Figure 2   Residential energy prices, 1907-1976   8

Figure 3   Industrial energy prices, 1950-1975   9

Figure 4   Predicted energy savings for several thermostat settings   10

Figure 5   Energy flow for a gas furnace system   12

Figure 6   Residential gas conservation   13

Figure 7   Space heating thermal integrity for single-family units versus increased capital costs   14

Figure 8   Electricity use versus retail price for a typical refrigerator   16

Figure 9   The automobile   20

Figure 10   Total energy consumption, historical and projected   22

Figure 11   Per capita energy, historical and projected   24

Figure 12   Energy per $ GNP, historical and projected   26

x   List of Figures

Chapter 2

Figure 1   Year 2000 energy and GNP   32

Figure 2   GSP/E or GDP/E versus E/L for U.S. and
            foreign countries, 1971   34

Figure 3   Energy import dependence compared with
            energy/output ratios, 1972   35

Figure 4   Phases of R&D   38

Figure 5   Social costs of supply-demand mismatch
            for electricity   40

Figure 6   General form of the sigmoid curve   44

Figure 7   Output of power devices: 1700-2000   45

Figure 8   Illumination   46

Figure 9   Illumination trends   47

Figure 10   Annual resource depletion extrapolated
            from initial data and real world   48

Figure 11   Resource availability and costs with
            shifts due to technology   50

Figure 12   Estimated capital costs and capital
            charges for new electricity options   52

Figure 13   Allowable area related costs of al-
            ternative solar system concepts (1976
            dollars)   54

Chapter 6

Figure 1   The elasticity of substitution concept   142

Figure 2   Economic impacts of energy reductions
            in the year 2010 for various elastici-
            ties of substitution   143

Figure 3   U.S. time series of crude oil prices
            and fossil energy/GNP ratios   146

Figure 4   An international comparison of energy/
            GNP ratios in 1973   148

List of Figures   *xi*

Chapter 7

Figure 1   Average price and replacement cost
             of oil and other existing energy
             sources from 1950 to mid-1976   154

Figure 2   Supply of "conservation energy"
             residential gas users -- California   162

List of Tables and Charts

Chapter 1

Table   1   Energy efficiencies in 2010, assuming
            real energy price doubles over the
            period   18

Chapter 2

Table   1   Year 2000 end-use conservation poten-
            tial percent savings; Year 2000
            reasonable energy conservation poten-
            tial   30

Table   2   Ranking of factors affecting comparative
            energy consumption/GDP ratios, 1972   37

Chapter 3

Table   1   Per capita income as percent of U.S.
            total, by regions: 1840-1975   68

Chart   1   Projection of demand and capacity in
            OPEC production   74

Table   2   Various 1985 projections of domestic
            energy production and shortfalls
            relative to NEP goals and requirements   76

Chart   2   Lead times in domestic energy development   78

Chart   3   Cyclical behavior of non-residential
            investment in seven major countries,
            1955-1978   82

xiii

xiv   List of Tables and Charts

Table 3	Gross private domestic investment as a proportion of GNP: Selected years	86
Table 4	U.S. energy investment, 1977–1985, to fulfill 1985 NEP targets	89
Table 5	Estimated energy investment, 1977–1985, to fulfill 1985 NEP targets	92
Table 6	Annual average percentage growth in real earnings by regions: 1971–1976; Percentage population change between 1970 and 1975	96
Table 7	Energy production capital requirements by regions to 1985: Nine years	99
Table 8	Energy production capital requirements by sector to 1985: Nine years	100
Table 9	Energy conservation investment by regions, 1977–1985	102
Table 10	Total 1977–1985 regional energy investment; per household; and per dollar value-added in manufacturing	103

Chapter 4

Chart 1	BTU per dollar of gross domestic product (1972 dollars), 1927–1976	114
Table 1	Per capita energy consumption and per capita gross domestic product, nine developed countries, 1972	120

Chapter 7

Table 1	Average price and replacement cost of energy used in industry	156
Table 2	Composite of preliminary findings: The Major Technologies	164

About the Editor and Authors

Charles J. Hitch, president of Resources for the Future in Washington, D.C., was formerly president of the University of California, and served as Assistant Secretary of Defense (Comptroller) from 1961-1965. He was also chairman of the General Advisory Committee of the Energy Research and Development Administration and vice president of the American Economic Association. A fellow of the American Association for the Advancement of Science, of the American Academy of Arts and Sciences, and of the Econometric Society, he has also been awarded numerous honorary degrees. He has published several books on various aspects of economics, including Modeling Energy-Economy Interactions: Five Approaches *(Resources for the Future, 1977).*

Joel Darmstadter, a fellow at the Center for Energy Policy Research, Resources for the Future, is also a member of the Demand/Conservation Panel of the National Academy of Sciences' Committee on Nuclear and Alternative Energy Systems, and a consultant to the Office of Technology Assessment. His work has focused on the economic aspects of energy demand, and he is the author of numerous books and articles including How Industrial Societies Use Energy: A Comparative Analysis *(with J. Dunkerley and J. Alterman; Johns Hopkins University Press/Resources for the Future, 1977).*

John H. Gibbons, director of the University of Tennessee Environment Center and a professor of physics at the University, was previously director of the Office of Energy Conservation, Federal Energy Administration. He is chairman of a number of panels on energy issues at the National Academy of Sciences and the Office of Technology Assessment, a member of the advisory committees on energy and policy issues of numerous organizations, and a member of the board of editors for Energy Systems and Policy. *He is a recipient of*

xv

xvi   About the Editor and Authors

the Distinguished Service Award of the FEA and the author of numerous publications in the areas of energy and environmental policy; energy supply and demand, conservation, technology, and policy; and related subjects.

Denis Hayes, senior researcher at Worldwatch Institute in Washington, D.C., is concerned with energy, environment, and natural resources policy. He is a member of the Board of Directors of the Federation of American Scientists, Environmental Action Foundation, Urban Environment Foundation, and Solar Action, Inc., and was formerly director of the Illinois State Energy Office. He has written six books including **Rays of Hope: The Transition to a Post-Petroleum World** *(W.W. Norton, 1977) and* **Energy: The Case for Conservation** *(Worldwatch Institute, 1976).*

Alan S. Manne, professor of operations research at Stanford University, specializes in energy, environmental, and economic modeling and is the author of several papers in these areas. He is a fellow of the Econometric Society and was awarded the Lanchester Prize of the Operations Research Society of America.

W. W. Rostow, professor of economics and history at the University of Texas at Austin, served under Presidents Kennedy and Johnson as Deputy Special Assistant for National Security Affairs, and under President Kennedy in the Department of State as counselor and chairman of the Policy Planning Council. He was awarded the Presidential Medal of Freedom with distinction in 1969. Professor Rostow is the author of some 20 books, most recently, **How It All Began: The Origins of Modern Economic Growth** *(McGraw-Hill, 1975) and* **The World Economy: History and Prospect** *(1978).*

Roger W. Sant, director of the Energy Conservation Policy Center at the Carnegie-Mellon Institute of Research, has written numerous papers and articles on energy conservation and related topics. He is a member of the Advisory Council of the Gas Research Institute and was formerly assistant administrator at the Federal Energy Administration.

Chauncey Starr, president of the Electric Power Research Institute, was previously dean of the UCLA School of Engineering and Applied Science and vice president of Rockwell International. He is a member and past vice president of the National Academy of Engineering, founder and past president of the American Nuclear Society, and a director of the American Association for the Advancement of Science. He is the author of numerous publications in engineering, energy, and related fields.

Introduction

Charles J. Hitch

The subject of this volume goes to the heart of the continuing debate on national energy policy. In adjusting to more costly energy sources (which all the authors expect), how much should we rely on conserving energy and how much on increasing its supply? The special focus of this volume is the impact of energy conservation on economic growth: is it positive, negative, or neutral?

Each author agrees that higher energy costs in themselves will have some damping effect on growth, how much depending on many factors. Can conservation mitigate this effect, and if so, what kind and how much conservation, and how achieved? Here disagreements among the authors begin to emerge, with varying shades of optimism and pessimism about the potential role of conservation represented, as well as some agnosticism. The most optimistic see in energy constraints an opportunity--if we have the wit to seize it-- for achieving via conservation simpler, cleaner life styles; or for resuscitating a stagnant, underemployed economy by investment in conservation as well as supply technologies. Even the pessimistic assign some role to conservation, albeit a limited one; they stress the need for increased energy supplies as well to fuel the economic growth they consider necessary to achieve many other national and international objectives. The agnostics (and all the authors are to some degree agnostic) call for more research. To be fair, they do not merely call for it; some describe in detail what research is needed to make better informed decisions.

John Gibbons ("The Imperative of Energy Conservation for Economic Growth") provides a taxonomy of conservation responses to scarcities and rising prices. Combining engineering and economic analyses he argues that very large economies in energy use are achievable, but that most require new capital and much time, technological sophistication

2   *Introduction*

(rather than a return to Thoreau's Walden), and getting energy price signals straight -- to reflect non-market as well as full market costs. Conservation is essential not only to our economic growth, but to our economic survival in a competitive world.

Chauncey Starr ("The Consistency of Economic Growth and Energy Conservation Technology") is impressed by the historically close coupling of energy and Gross National Product, and is therefore much more cautious in assessing the potential of cost-effective conservation. His answer to the question "Can technology permit the simultaneous achievement of economic growth and conservation objectives"? is "Yes, up to a point, but there are time lags in achieving the benefits of technological change, and some dangers in relying too heavily on energy conservation technology as a means of reducing energy consumption".

Walt Rostow ("Energy and Full Employment") is unwilling to limit himself to asking how little energy and how much conservation are consistent with economic growth. He goes on to question whether a balanced U.S. energy production and conservation program itself could bring about conditions of full employment and accelerated growth. Because regions of the country differ so greatly in unemployment rates, energy resource endowments, and potentialities for conservation, he pursues his question region by region as well as for the U.S. economy in the aggregate. His answers, with important qualifications, are affirmative.

Joel Darmstadter ("Lessons of History and Other Countries") first examines our own economic history, where he observes substantial decoupling of energy and economic activity. Since the mid-1920's, for example, U.S. energy use in relation to real GNP has declined by about 20 percent in spite of the fact that real energy prices were steadily falling until 1970. Comparisons with other industrial countries, while tricky to interpret and sometimes interpreted simplistically, confirm this loose relation. Intercountry comparisons also suggest (such statistics can "prove" nothing) that energy demand and use are quite sensitive in the long run to energy prices.

Denis Hayes ("Post-Petroleum Prosperity") is the most optimistic of the authors on the prospects for conservation and decoupling. He expects the energy sources replacing oil to be more expensive, but is convinced by analysis as well as by the Japanese and European experiences that a healthy economy can co-exist with high energy prices. Materials, labor, and especially human ingenuity can be substituted for

Introduction   3

expensive fuel. Because the need for conservation investment is so large in relation to available capital, and is more cost effective and environmentally benign than investment in increasing energy supply, it should be given an overriding priority.

Alan Manne ("The Fable of the Elephant and the Rabbit?") identifies the critical factors in determining the impact of energy prices and availability on future GNP to be: the relative size of the primary energy section (it is now small-5 or so percent of GNP) and the ease with which other factors of production--labor, materials and capital--can be substituted for energy. If cost/effective substitution possibilities are great, we can adapt--if we have time--to substantially higher prices (or reduced availabilities) of energy with little pain. If the possibilities are slight, the effects on economic growth could be very damaging. Unfortunately, we don't know the numerical values of the relevant elasticities. In these circumstances it would be imprudent to rely too heavily on conservation and neglect opportunities to enhance supplies.

Roger Sant ("Adjusting Capital Stock to Higher Energy Using Efficiencies") describes the current debate over how much energy is required for a given level of economic activity as interesting but inconclusive, like a religious argument. So he attempts, in effect, to outline a process-oriented research program to determine those numerical values which Manne needs to settle the argument. His very tentative results are that almost $220 billion of capital investment (in industry, commercial buildings, residences, and transportation) would be cost/effective at current marginal costs of energy, and that this would save about 20 quadrillion BTU's of 1985 energy use. Further research is necessary for a good estimate of how much of that investment would actually be made by 1985, given behavioral inertia and institutional obstacles.

As chairman of the AAAS session at which these papers were presented and discussed, and editor of this volume, I have been intrigued by the question: How much real disagreement is there in this diverse group of authors? My belief is that there is much less than there would have been two years ago or even one year ago. Research and analysis has made progress in improving our understanding of energy problems, and the participants are listening more and shouting less. (Of course, this doesn't necessarily mean that they have become more successful in influencing policy.)

4 Introduction

Some of the areas of agreement are now so taken for granted that they do not emerge as major themes in any of the papers. All agree that conservation has a major role to play; that no longer has to be argued. All agree that the "right kind" of conservation, far from being a "sacrifice", mitigates the impact of energy constraints on economic growth. All agree that the right kind is that which is cost effective at replacement cost (including "externalities"). And I believe all agree that this right kind of conservation should be induced, in the main, by markets in which prices are giving appropriate signals, although some would prefer regulation in certain cases, and others think special inducements or subsidies are necessary beyond the R and D stage to get some new technologies commercialized. Of course, past and present controlled prices have been giving inappropriate, even perverse, messages to consumers at all levels.

Some of the differences may be more apparent than real. Looking at the same historical data, Darmstadter examines the ratio of total annual energy consumption to annual GNP and finds that it has decreased over time; whereas Starr emphasizes that the same data display almost a straight line relationship during the past 75 years. Both can be right about the past.

But there are real differences. One is the degree of agnosticism regarding the ease of substitutability. Manne counsels caution; Gibbons and Hayes express great confidence. Not surprisingly other differences relate to values and policy prescriptions. Rostow, for example, deeply concerned about stagnation and unemployment, wants all the investment he can get, whether for enhanced energy supply or energy conservation. Hayes, impressed by the negative externalities of fossil fuels and nuclear and fearful of "crowding out," would put all energy investment into conservation and new "soft" technologies.

It is time to let the authors speak for themselves.

1

The Imperative of Energy Conservation for Economic Growth

John H. Gibbons

At the beginning of this decade we witnessed some indications of looming energy shortages: there was mounting dependence on imports, and we had such portents as the six-miles-per-gallon car and 15 percent annual growth in airplane transportation. Mixed with that situation were escalating environmental problems and rapidly spreading environmental awareness.

Of course, what we didn't foresee at that time was the sharply increasing price for energy in the years ahead. The notion of conservation of energy was discussed by only a few people and even fewer understood what they were talking about or agreed with each other. Serious attention to demand was spawned not by low MPG cars or other indicators of that period but by the Yom Kippur War in October, 1973. In a way, it is fortunate that our consciousness was triggered when it was, for had it not been it might have been many years before we came to a more direct confrontation of the problem. However, at the same time it was unfortunate that the embargo was the event that so impressed us, for "conservation" became intimately linked not with a long-term move in response to an economic and national security imperative, but rather to an emergency and traumatic curtailment in response to a momentary interruption of some of our petroleum supplies.

Figure 1 describes those various activities that can be undertaken to moderate the demand for energy in general and particularly for certain energy supplies. Of the three strategies listed across the top, <u>curtailment</u> is a series of heroic measures taken in the face of emergencies, such as the winter of 1973-74, and the coal strikes of 1975 and 1977-78. <u>Fuel switching</u> is a strategy simply to use less of a scarce resource and therefore more of some other energy resource. This is an important set of options, defensibly classifiable as conservation though not saving energy, per se. The third

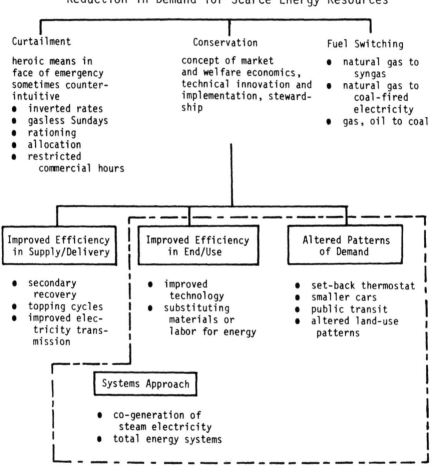

Figure 1

Reduction in Demand for Scarce Energy Resources

strategy, on which I'd like to focus, is <u>conservation</u> --
the concept of a rational economic response to true total
cost of the commodity of energy. In this sense, cost is
meant to imply both market price and other costs that do not
necessarily appear in the price.

Let me begin with two concepts important in any discussion of conserving energy -- "efficiency" and "waste".
One can certainly improve the efficiency in the end use of
energy, mostly by substituting capital for energy consumption. Also, of course, one may improve efficiency in the
supply system itself: more efficient power plants make a
given energy resource stretch that much further. There are
also conservation opportunities that interact and intersect
between supply and end use in such areas as total energy
utilization and cogeneration of heat and electricity.
Another conservation strategy -- altered patterns of demand--
categorizes those actions one takes in the use of income to
maximize personal benefits. When the price of energy goes
up with respect to other goods and commodities, we shift in
our behavior patterns to take account of that change.

In the context of economics, waste is not a thing in-
and-of itself: if energy is free, there is no waste. On the
other hand, as cost goes up, things that are not wasteful
today may be wasteful tomorrow. Waste is an economic term
and it changes with the situation.

Figure 2 summarizes changes that have occurred in energy
price. Two features should be noted: one is the sharp change
in 1973, but the second is that the real price of energy
since that sharp upturn has not changed appreciably. In the
case of gasoline, the price has returned to the level of the
late 1950's. It is surprising to many, but we're not so much
in a new era of price as we are back to an old era of price.

Figure 3 shows what has happened to energy prices in the
industrial sector. Obviously, some prices are up more than
others; indeed, some have only returned to their post-World
War II levels. Because these prices have only moved back to
some of their older levels, the response to this new price
change, in and of itself, may not be terribly strong or rapid.
The price signal just isn't that strong. Furthermore, price
in the last year has actually decreased for some of these
energy commodities.

How far might market prices go up in the future? And
over what time? What are the real energy costs of various
things we do with energy if we stripped away price controls,
subsidies, and actually incorporated all of the identifiable

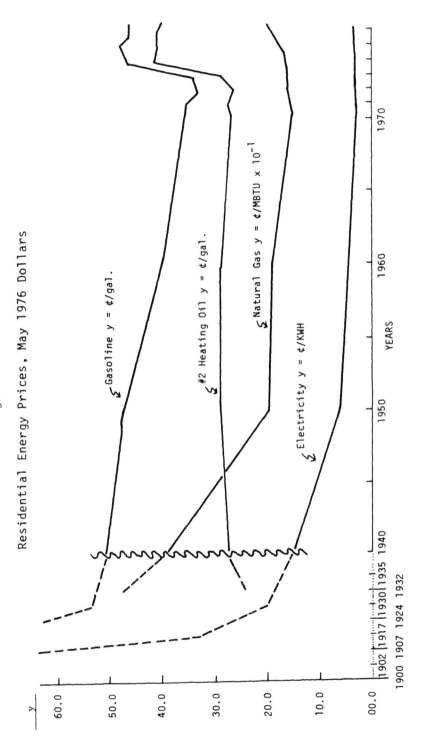

Figure 2

Residential Energy Prices, May 1976 Dollars

Figure 3

Industrial Energy Prices

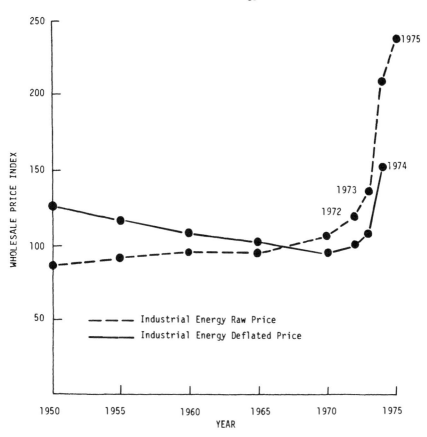

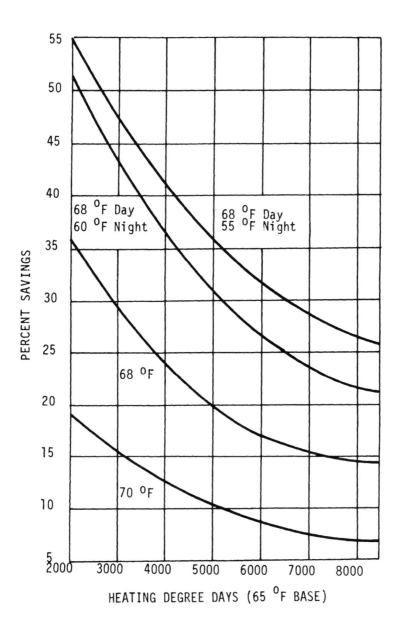

Fig. 4. Predicted energy savings for several thermostat settings (72°F is the reference setting and night setback is from 10 PM to 6 AM).

social costs and national security costs associated with energy? What would be the response to a continued price rise? And what would be the new system of prices, of utilization patterns, that would derive from this kind of price trend? How would the altered supply and the consumption rates that result from this affect employment, equity, and economic growth?

There are various approaches to the analysis of this situation. There are macroeconomic approaches, microeconomic analysis approaches, speculation (sometimes as good as anything else), engineering analyses, and hybrids, particularly in engineering analysis and microeconomic analysis. For the purposes of this paper, my focus is on end use, using a little hybrid engineering and microeconomics plus some vignettes of end use.

There are three kinds of responses that can be made to a situation of rising cost and scarcity. First is behavior modification. Figure 4 does not look like a behavior modification chart, but it serves to indicate the kind of savings one can attain simply by turning the dial of a thermostat, a simple and easily available behavior modification and a typical short-term response to a change in energy price or availability. There are only a few things one can do in the near-term wake of a sudden change; one is to turn down dials and the other is to use the energy-consuming equipment less. The short-term objective is simply to try to mitigate the overall economic hardship of a traumatic and emergency situation.

The second response is to modify existing energy-consuming equipment. When one analyzes where heat goes in a house once it leaves the furnace (Figure 5), one finds that between stack loss and duct loss there is a tremendous amount of energy lost simply because of non-energy conserving design and poor insulation. As shown in Figure 6, there are many things that can be done in the home, from showerhead flow restrictors to the insulation of water heaters, attics, floors, walls, and windows. The marginal return for each of these retrofit investments, or reinvestments in existing capital stock, is different. The return on investment can range all the way from extremely high benefit-to-cost to rather less attractive or even unattractive benefit-to-cost, depending upon the cost of energy. In fact, as in everything else, there are conservation actions one can take which result in losing money.

Figure 7 sums up a study of things that can be done in single-family residences in terms of energy intensiveness

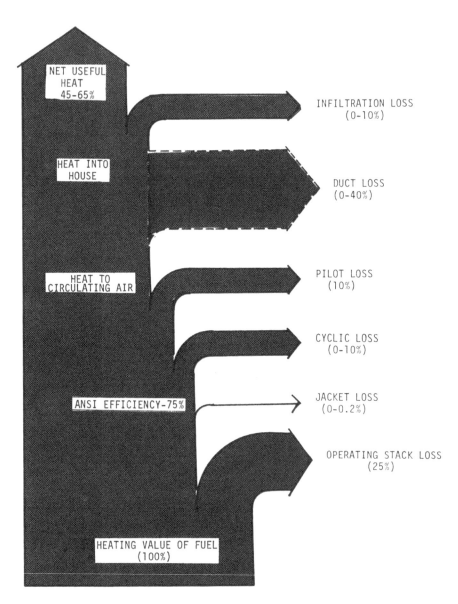

Fig. 5. Energy flow for a gas furnace system.

The Imperative of Conservation for Growth   13

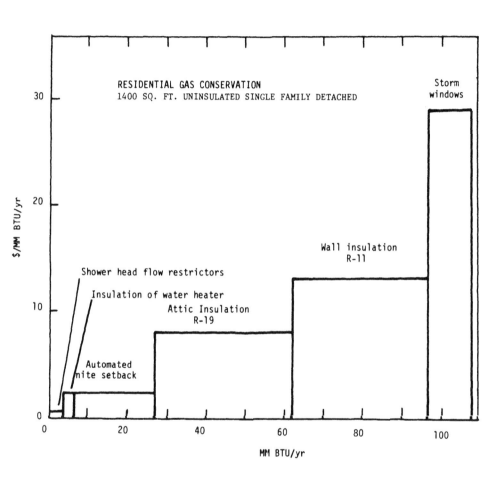

Figure 6

Residential Gas Conservation

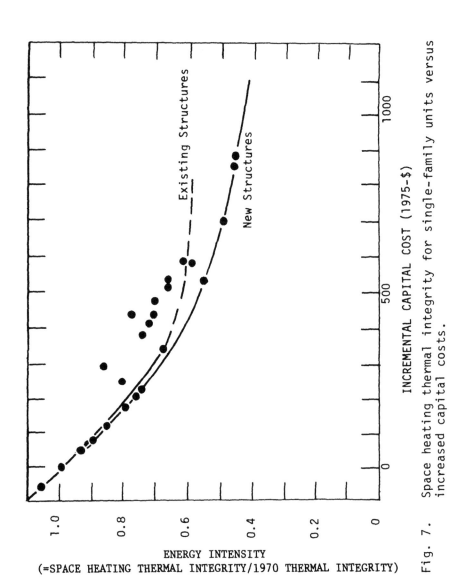

Fig. 7. Space heating thermal integrity for single-family units versus increased capital costs.

The Imperative of Conservation for Growth   15

versus increased capital investment. As indicated, the energy intensiveness for additional investment of a typical house can be decreased to about .6 or .7 in exchange for a relatively small incremental cost. Note also that in new houses (as opposed to existing houses), for the same amount of investment one can get a little better performance. It is simply easier to incorporate energy efficiency when constructing a house than when retrofitting it. In other areas of end use retrofitting is more difficult still. For example, it's very difficult to do much about an existing refrigerator.

So there are some things one can do to modify existing equipment. The modification can take anything from a few months to a few years to achieve. In the case of retrofitting most of the United States' homes, perhaps a decade or maybe slightly longer will be required even with a vigorous program.

In the industrial sector, it is remarkable how many things can be done. The February 9, 1978, issue of the Wall Street Journal carried a progress report on actions being taken in the industrial sector across the country, not so much in the development of new industrial processes, for that takes decades, but in the modification of existing processes in order to save money. Three examples: $30,000 was spent for a set of boiler controls, and the company's fuel savings from this investment is $60,000 a year, a 200 percent annual return; $40,000 was spent to insulate some steam valves in a tire manufacturing plant -- the return is $80,000 a year, or another 200 percent; $13,000 was spent by General Electric in a manufacturing plant to put in some automatic timers to shut down certain pieces of equipment. The $13,000 investment resulted in a $51,000 a year savings.

Of course, these are the easy ones: the conservation investments turn out to be far more profitable than the products the companies are trying to sell. There seems to be a great number of these opportunities, so many that it appears, nonsensically, that one could turn a profit by not making any product! But realistically, who knows what might happen if we began to make investments that have returns all the way down to, say, 10 percent per year? The modification of existing energy-consuming capital equipment is a process that has cost-effective opportunities in every sector of energy use. Virtually all of these take some capital, and they obviously also require time, but the overall magnitude of opportunity is very large indeed.

The third kind of response to price and scarcity is the modification of energy intensiveness of new capital equipment.

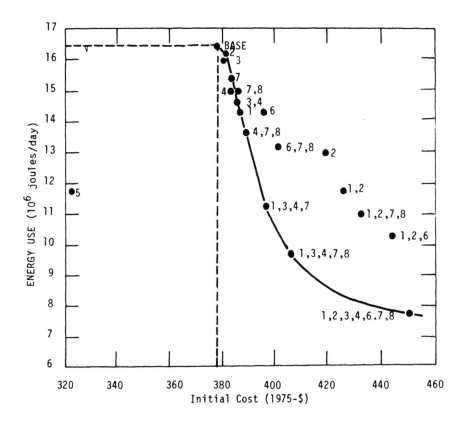

Fig. 8. Electricity use versus retail price for a typical refrigerator.

1 Increase insulation thickness
2 Improve insulation thermal conductivity
3 Remove fan from cooled area
4 Add anti-sweat heater switch
5 Eliminate frost-free and forced air systems
6 Improve compressor efficiency
7 Increase condenser surface area
8 Increase evaporator surface area

As noted above, it is in new structures that one finds tremendous changes in energy requirements that can be achieved through careful design and construction. It also turns out that the *gross* investment to install, for example, double-paned glass and much greater insulation and many other energy conserving investments, is partially offset by the reduced size, and therefore, cost of the air conditioner or the furnace required; the costs trade off, one against the other. That is the reason one can get such large improvements in energy intensiveness for such small *net* changes in prices of total cost.

Let us look at the refrigerator (Figure 8). The abscissa graphs initial cost in 1975 dollars and the ordinate is energy intensiveness. Note that with relatively small net changes in capital cost for the refrigerator, one finds rapidly decreasing energy intensiveness. The break-even point at present typical energy costs is probably at an energy-intensiveness somewhere between 0.5 and 0.6 (i.e., about one half) of the average refrigerator as shown indicated by the dotted line. As one adds considerable capital investments to the refrigerator the curve begins to flatten out, indicating that the marginal return in that investment is diminishing, that it takes more and more expensive energy to justify making the refrigerator any more efficient. There are similar curves for air conditioners and for other energy-intensive appliances.

Table I presents results of some work by the panel on Demand and Conservation for the National Research Council's Committee on Nuclear and Alternative Energy Systems. It is the result of a study of the scenario that examined what would happen to industrial energy efficiency in 2010 as a result of steady progression of the *real* price of energy at an average rate of some two percent per year, a rate which corresponds to a doubling of real price over that period of time. One finds that various industries would respond in different ways to such a price trend and that the energy intensiveness of production (energy consumed per unit of output) would decrease as little as about 20 percent in the chemical sector but much more in other sectors.

In developing this scenario, one must assume that industry perceives the long-term upward price ramp. Of course, that is not necessarily the case. Also note that much time is required for such an industrial response; and these numbers obtain only over a period of several decades. The actual time required for this kind of response is dependent on the rate of economic growth or some assumed policy measure such as an increase in investment tax credit. Higher

Table 1

Energy Efficiencies in 2010,
Assuming Real Energy Price Doubles Over the Period

Buildings and Appliances		Industry		Transportation	
Type	Intensity[(a)]	Type	Intensity[(b)]	Type	Intensity[(d)]
Thermal integrity (heating)		Agriculture	.85	Automobile	27 mpg
- residential	.63	Aluminum	.63	Light trucks, Vans	21 mpg
- commercial	.6	Cement	.63	Air passenger	.45
- government/education	.45	Chemicals	.78[(c)]	Truck freight	.8
Space conditioning		Construction	.65	Air freight	.6
- air condition	.75	Food	.76	Rail freight	.97
- electric heating	.63	Glass	.76		
- gas, oil heating	.75	Iron & Steel	.76		
Refrigeration, freezing	.68	Paper	.71		
Lighting	.70	Other Industry	.75		

(a) Energy-intensity of new construction and products in 2010 compared with 1975.

(b) Average energy per unit production in 2010 compared with 1975.

(c) Excluding feedstock.

(d) When figures are not given in designated units they refer to energy-intensity in 2010 compared with 1975 (including changes in load factor).

economic growth means greater product demand and therefore new plant commitment and more efficient plants. Investments in conservation may be very cost-effective, but that fact alone normally will not cause an industry to justify building a new plant.

There is also a very important point raised by Charles Berg in _Science_.[1] Berg points out that in addition to using more effectively the kinds of technology that we have available today, major changes in the price or availability of energy undoubtedly will trigger innovation in the industrial sector. For example, Berg notes that it appears to be possible that ceramics production can be done at low temperature, rather than extremely high temperature, using catalytic chemical reactions. If true, this indicates how entirely new processes can sharply reduce energy requirements. Another example is the centrifuge process for uranium separation which requires only 10 percent of the energy required by the present gaseous diffusion process.

The automobile is the subject of Figure 9, with the dotted and solid lines representing two different assumptions about gasoline price. The abscissa is the economy of the automobile (miles per gallon increases to the right). The ordinate is the car's operating cost, of which there are two kinds. One is to provide gas and oil, and those costs go down with a more efficient car. The second cost is that associated with ownership itself, including purchase payments, insurance, license, etc. If one wants the same amenities (in terms of interior seating space, safety, and other essential features) but also a more energy-efficient automobile, micro-processors and a lot of other high-technology materials and devices must be added to achieve that efficiency; therefore the price goes up. Those two kinds of cost added together are the "total cost" to own and operate—the inverted bell shaped curve. The very low mileage car uses so much gas and oil that it costs more than many people want to pay. On the other hand, the very high efficiency car may cost so much initially that one cannot justify the expense through the savings of gas and oil. Notice that the total cost curve has a minimum with a very interesting feature: the total cost is nearly insensitive to the performance of the car over a broad range from 15 miles per gallon up to nearly 35 miles per gallon. If the purchaser of the automobile receives even a perfect market signal of

---

[1] "Conservation In Industry", _Science_, Vol. 184, April 19, 1974, pp. 264-270.

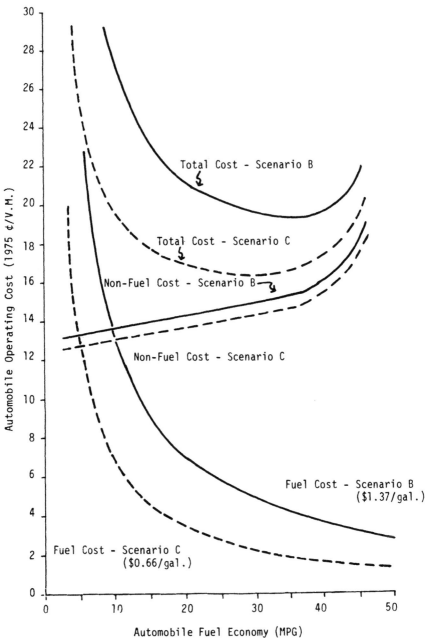

Figure 9

The Automobile

The Imperative of Conservation for Growth 21

total cost and therefore is a totally informed buyer, he still doesn't know whether to choose the 15 or the 35 mpg car. Clearly, if total cost is rather insensitive to energy efficiency, it really does not make that much difference to the consumer. But one probably can claim that it is in the national interest to choose the most efficient purchase, at least in terms of spending money on imported oil vs. spending money domestically to build more sophisticated automobiles. What we witness here is not so much a market **failure** as an **insufficiency** of the market process to enable consumers to make the nationally most efficient choice.

In summary, careful engineering analysis indicates that considerably more efficient devices are achievable and economically feasible even at today's energy prices, but most of the opportunities to achieve these more efficient devices require time, the sort of time characteristic of capital stock turnover. Refrigerators last 15 years, automobiles last a decade, houses last 30 years or more, industrial plants last one-half a century or more, and it is only in that kind of time frame that we find our greatest opportunities. Thus, the argument that changing efficiency of energy in our society is a little like silly putty: if you try to stretch it too fast it snaps, but if you stretch it slowly you can alter its shape and form quite considerably. Thermodynamic limits are far from present practice in energy consumption.

A second observation is that technological sophistication is required to obtain conservation. An energy-efficient society does not imply an embracing of Thoreau's Walden but instead will require a full utilization of human ingenuity through technology to achieve this efficiency. Technological sophistication will result in investments in energy-utilization capital and labor as substitutes for energy purchases, nuclear power plant construction, coal mining, and other investments on the supply side.

What about labor substitution? Does a conservation move toward high efficiency mean a return to men and women pushing wheelbarrows again, as one financial observer has indicated? A moment's deliberation can dispel that notion. Ten to twenty cents worth of electricity buys at least one man day of the wheelbarrow-pushing type of labor just about anywhere in the United States. Clearly any conceivable energy price is not going to provide an economic argument to substitute wheelbarrows for bulldozers! The kind of labor associated with the conservation program described herein is not manual labor but rather electronics technicians, skilled construction workers, engineers, and others who can help

Figure 10*

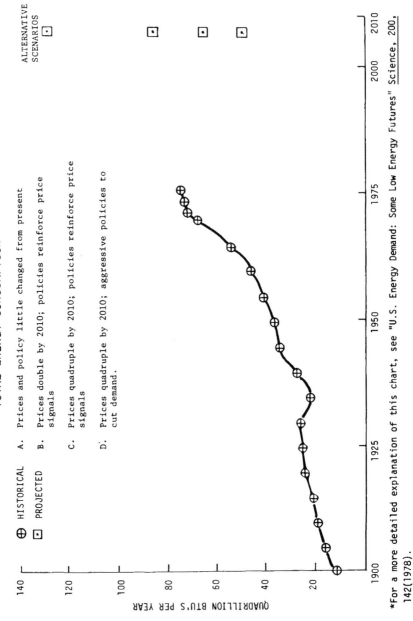

*For a more detailed explanation of this chart, see "U.S. Energy Demand: Some Low Energy Futures" Science, 200, 142(1978).

The Imperative of Conservation for Growth 23

substitute ingenuity for brute-force energy consumption.

I want to repeat my earlier observation about the trade-off between energy efficiency and total cost to own and operate energy-consuming investments. It is essential to remember that the total cost of energy consuming devices that deliver roughly the same amenity is rather insensitive to efficiency. Because the sensitivity is typically so low we find that the market is insufficient in guiding the consumer to make wise purchase choices.

A fourth observation has to do with economic imperatives for conservation. If our aim in society is to provide maximal amenities for a given investment of capital, labor, and materials, and if the costs are less to save a unit of energy than to provide that same unit of energy, then the investment should be made in saving rather than providing. If a barrel of oil can be saved productively with $10 worth of U.S. materials and labor instead of being bought for $12 from foreign markets, which choice would you take? It seems to me that when we come to the issue of "how much conservation" we can afford, the answer is, as much as rational economic analysis tells us we should afford. In this regard, we must take into account not only traditional market costs but also other, non-market, costs.

A fifth observation: in contrast to expenditures for pollution control (which surely have benefits, although these are social), investments in conservation generally are productive in both private benefits and social benefits. We are far from exceeding private benefits in our conservation investments up to now.

My sixth and last observation has to do with the issue of "insurance", because I think we are dealing with great uncertainties. Energy systems, whether for supply or use, have a characteristic time constant measured in decades. We therefore need to make decisions now to significantly influence the system 10, 20, or 30 years hence. Because the future is so dimly perceived, should we not plan to build "extra" capacity even if we are unsure whether we need it? Similarly, should we not build spare efficiency into our energy utilization system well beyond the point that current energy prices dictate? I believe the answer is that we probably need to invest in all areas where the investment required to gain that insurance costs us the least amount of extra money today.

Figure 10 summarizes total energy consumption in the United States up to 1976. Generally the analyses range from

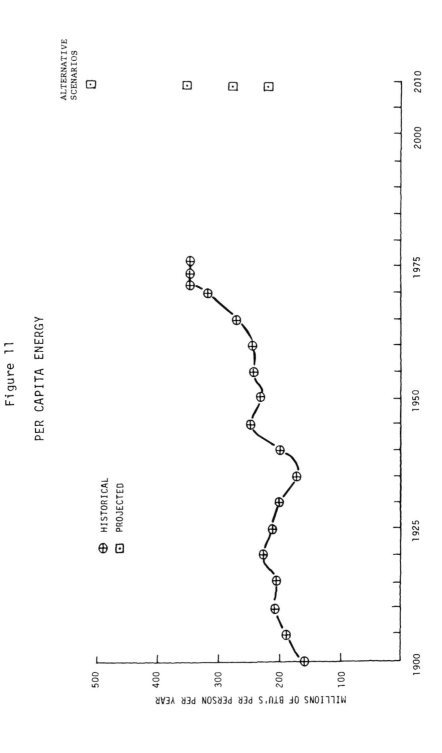

The Imperative of Conservation for Growth   25

about 70 quads up to about 150 quads in 2010. In the early 1970's the notion was that 2010 consumption would be in the range from 200 to 300 quads. Of course, the consensus has since been grossly modified. Figure 11 removes the role of population growth during this same time period and displays energy consumed per capita.

Figure 12 gives the long-term trend in the ratio of energy divided by GNP for the United States. Note there has been a substantial decrease in this ratio, largely reflecting the advance of technology in energy utilization. During the period up to 1970 this improvement occurred during an era of decreasing real energy price. In future years, with increasing energy price and supporting public policy, it is quite likely that the long-term trend to higher efficiency will continue.

A recent cartoon depicting two scientists hard at work reads, "What's most depressing is the realization that everything we believe will be disproved within a few years." We presume -- or ought to -- that the future holds this fate for us. Market imperfections may be overcome with additional signals such as regulation and minimum performance criteria, but we are a society that doesn't like to think or plan very far ahead. Adlai Stevenson once said that "we never seem to see the handwriting on the wall until our back is up against it".

In facing the energy problem we are concerned with issues that challenge much of our traditional thinking: dualism (homo sapiens vs. the rest of nature) and the "cowboy economy". Under these notions, nature is present simply to serve human pleasures; furthermore, nature is infinite, so to solve problems we either move West or make more or do a little bit of both!

I believe that vigorous conservation is essential not only to our economic growth but also to our economic survival in a competitive world. This kind of conservation implies major, long-term shifts of capital investment to the energy-consuming sectors. There is a need to clarify energy price signals. The present energy market is highly distorted due to energy price subsidies, from natural gas to river transportation. There is a great need to strip away subsidies and controls, layer by layer, in order to more nearly perfect the market. Nor are these market distortions all ancient history. In a new subsidy established in 1977 we pay out of general tax revenues for the creation of our strategic petroleum reserves. Other countries -- for example, Israel -- pay for such storage out of a tax on petroleum users.

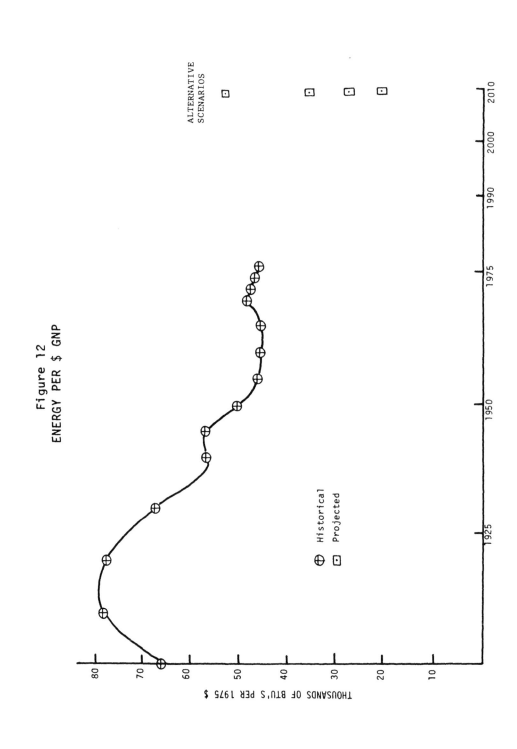

Figure 12
ENERGY PER $ GNP

The Imperative of Conservation for Growth   27

Nature's limits on efficiency of energy use are far from being met. There is much that human ingenuity can do, given the chance to work. Higher prices for energy give us that chance, for the response to price can be a substitution of domestic resources and labor for more expensive, foreign purchases. Therefore, my claim is that conservation actions wisely chosen aid employment as well as sustain our domestic economic strength.

Despite the opportunities, our conservation goals will not be achieved without public policies to make the total cost of energy more visible, through price, taxation or regulation. The "hidden hand" of the free market needs to be more visible if we would have it work to efficiently allocate these resources. Max Born once said that "intellect distinguishes between the possible and the impossible; reason distinguishes between the sensible and the senseless; even the possible can be senseless". I believe that the issue of ought, can and will is at the core of the long-term energy situation. We may be coming to a consensus about what probably ought to be done in energy utilization. I think that it is more and more clear what can be done with both energy supply and utilization. The issue before us yet to be resolved is: What in fact will we do about it?

2

The Consistency of Economic Growth and Energy Conservation Technology

Chauncey Starr

Introduction

Because it is with the economy we are concerned and the future "well being" of the members of this society, the focus of this paper is on the consistency of economic growth and energy conservation. It attempts to respond to the question: Does technology exist (now, or in the future) to meet economic growth and energy consumption objectives and can it be applied in time?

Historical evidence of the past few decades shows that the growth in our economic output has paralleled a similar increase in energy consumption. In fact, between 1950 and 1973, the economy grew at 3.6 percent per year while energy consumption grew at 3.4 percent per year. And it is natural to attribute a causal relationship to these patterns. If, therefore, abundant energy is assumed to be essential for future economic well being, a preparatory effort is required now to guarantee that our future needs are met. Of just what this effect is composed is an important question, of course, because a narrowly restricted number of future energy options might unavoidably also restrict energy availability.

Although the detailed structure of the clear link between energy and the economy is not completely understood,[1] we do know that basic natural processes require some energy for every activity, and if adequate energy is not available the activity cannot take place. From this perspective, the linkage of energy and the economy appears causal. Obviously, the quantitative relation can be altered by the changing efficiency with which primary energy is converted and used to produce economic goods. Such changes take place slowly because, in the near-term, we depend on the capital equipment and processes now in place and their range of energy utili-

Table 1

Year 2000 End-Use Conservation Potential
Percent Savings

CONSERVATION PROGRAM	ELECTRIC ENERGY SECTOR	NON-ELECTRIC ENERGY SECTOR	TOTAL ENERGY
None	0%	0%	0%
Reasonable	17%	25%	20%
Extreme	34%	50%	40%

Year 2000 Reasonable Energy Conservation Potential

	SECTOR IMPORTANCE (% of total energy)		POTENTIAL ENERGY SAVINGS (% of year 2000 sector energy demand)	WEIGHTED POTENTIAL ANNUAL SAVINGS (% of year 2000 unperturbed total energy demand)
	1975	2000 (unperturbed)		
Residential & Commercial	35	40	15	6
Industrial	39	40	15	6
Transportation	26	20	40	8
	100%	100%	70%	20%

zation has little flexibility. In the longer run, however, old capital is replaced with new and "better" capital, alternative transportation systems are designed, the mix of products change and new technology is introduced. We submit in this paper, that the introduction of new technologies is a major and perhaps the most important key both for resource-savings and for future improvements in the "well being" of this society.

Planning Target

Subject to some substantial and unanticipated changes in the lifestyle of our society, it is likely that the economic/energy coupling will continue in the future. Also, it can be expected that this coupling will be modified over time by purposeful conservation and the introduction of new technologies. We therefore need to project plausibly our future energy requirements, and to plan accordingly.

In setting a national planning target for total energy requirements by the year 2000, there are four important variables to consider: the productivity of labor, employment level, the impact of conservation, and the energy required to meet national air and water quality goals. Concerning employment, the Bureau of Labor forecasts a civilian work force of 119 million by the year 2000, up from about 85 million today. In our analysis, we have assumed a 4 percent unemployment level. We have also estimated that environmentally motivated air and water quality control measures will constitute 10 percent of the national energy demand.

In terms of conservation, a distinction between technological conservation that raises the efficiency with which primary fuels are converted into end use, and sociological conservation that requires changing national lifestyles and end-use patterns must be made. A detailed survey of the potential for technological conservation, funded by Electric Power Research Institute, comprehensively covered the components of principal end-use sectors.(2) Table 1 provides a condensed summation of the results, both by energy form and by using sector. Although a 40 percent reduction appears technically possible, the economic costs make a 20 percent projection a prudent expectation for conservation potential by the year 2000.

Sociological conservation, on the other hand, is to a large degree voluntary in nature. While various conservation actions fall into this category, such as reducing thermostats and the formation of car pools, they are difficult to measure let alone forecast. Thus, conservation of this type is not

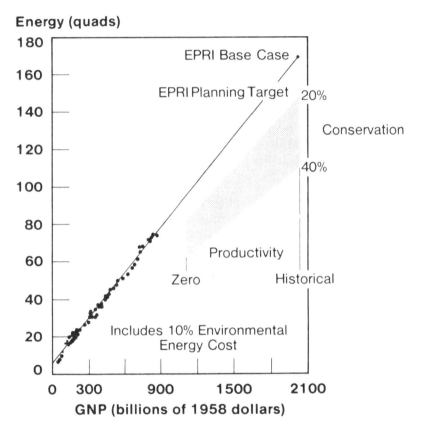

Figure 1 Year 2000 energy and GNP

included in the EPRI planning target. It should be emphasized that twenty five years is a short time for any sociologic trend to manifest a large cumulative effect on national
resource demand.

On the key assumption that economic growth will continue
unabated, Figure 1 shows a total energy requirement of 170
quads in the year 2000 if a linear projection of historical
data is made. The shaded trapezoid shows the range of projections that occur if the growth rate in the economic productivity of labor is varied between 0-2.3 (historical)
percent/year and conservation is varied between 20-40 percent
savings from the EPRI base case. We expect that actual
energy demand and GNP will fall near the top of this box.
This expectation makes sense if the lower left-hand corner
of the box is considered. Here in the year 2000 energy
demand is about 60 quads if 40 percent energy conservation
could be achieved and the productivity of labor was frozen
at today's values. The liklihood of this is quite low because of the economic and sociologic impact of such strong
constraints.

EPRI has selected the upper right-hand corner for prudent planning. That is, the planning target of 150 quads
assumes a reasonably achievable objective of 20 percent
conservation by the year 2000; 10 percent environmental
clean-up costs; continued historical growth in the productivity of labor; and a continued historical trend in our
changing labor force mix.

International Energy Comparisons
and Conservation Potential

Increasingly, references are being made to the comparison of energy use per unit of GDP of the U.S. to that of
Sweden, West Germany, and other developed countries as being
indicative of conservation potential. EPRI has been investigating this topic[3] and also commissioned Resources for
the Future to study how industrial societies use energy.[4]

In the EPRI paper, energy use patterns of each state of
the U.S. in relation to their individual economic output as
well as the energy intensity and income of their employed
workers are reviewed. The essense of the results is shown
in Figure 2. Several foreign countries, including Sweden
and West Germany are also shown. The key point is that for
any given level of average labor income, the ratio of energy
use to economic output is largely determined by the relative
availability of fuel, and the associated mix of economic
activities. This is also shown in Figure 3. Thus, it is

34 Chauncey Starr

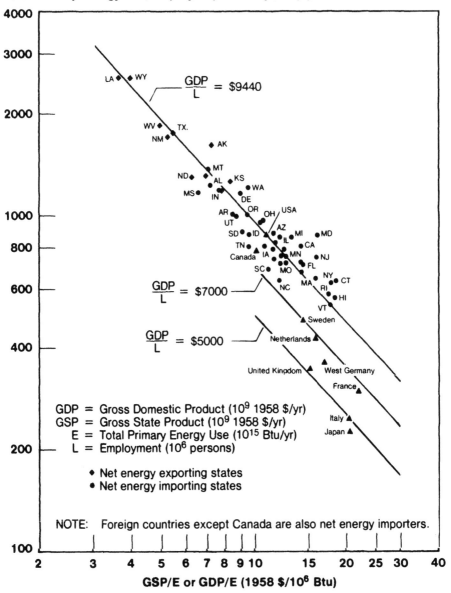

Figure 2 GSP/E or GDP/E versus E/L for U.S. and foreign countries, 1971

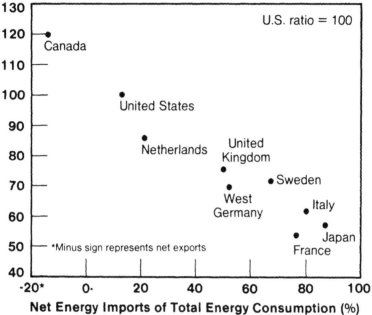

Figure 3   Energy import dependence compared with energy/output ratios, 1972

Source: J. Darmstadter, J. Dunkerley, and J. Alterman, *How Industrial Societies Use Energy: A Comparative Analysis* (Copyright ©The Johns Hopkins University Press for Resources for the Future, 1977)

clear that an energy/economic comparison does not provide a basis for comparing the energy conservation effectiveness of different countries. Certainly, no sweeping indictment of the U.S. is justified by such a comparison.

The RFF book endeavors to make clear the complexity of factors affecting differences in energy use and the difficulty of measuring efficiency and wastefulness. The authors try to do this by analyzing how much of the difference in energy use per dollar of national output among nine industrialized nations is attributable to, (1) the composition of a nation's output and activities (metallurgy and chemicals, for example, require a great deal of energy compared with light manufacturing); and (2) the amount of energy required in a partiuclar activity. What emerges is a sketch of the principal ingredients characterizing an energy-intensive economy: one nation's use of energy will be higher per dollar of output than another's when, for example, its relative fuel and power prices are lower; its passenger-mile volume is relatively larger; fuel economy of its passenger car fleet is poorer; housing units are larger and single dwelling units account for a larger share of housing; the industrial sector is relatively large and more energy intensive; the degree of self-sufficiency in energy supplies is greater. A ranking of countries according to some of these characteristics, Table 2, reflects this mixture.

New Technology Integration

Using 150 quads as a planning target, how long will it take to introduce new energy technologies? Historically, it has taken 30 to 45 years for a new technology to be developed and then achieve market penetration.

As shown in Figure 4, a new energy option must successfully pass through a number of development phases before significant use is achieved. That is, it moves from the simplest performance measure - "Will it work?" - to more difficult issues - "What is the best design from a viewpoint that includes considerations of cost, safety, environmental impacts, reliability and maintenance requirements?" Note that each development stage is significantly more costly than the previous stage as this figure indicates. This is largely due to the increasing size of the experiments, and the increasing amount of system integration which accompanies each phase.

Basically, the introduction of new technologies takes time, and there are pragmatic limits to speeding up this process. In turn, it can be slowed or stopped by administra-

Table 2

Ranking of Factors Affecting Comparative Energy Consumption/GDP Ratios, 1972

Factors	United States	Canada	France	West Germany	Italy	Netherlands	United Kingdom	Sweden	Japan
Energy prices (lowest prices = 1)	1	2	4	5	9	6	8	3	7
Passenger-miles per unit GDP	1	5	9	3	2	6	4	6	8
Percentage of passenger-miles accounted for by cars	1	2	8	4	7	5	6	3	9
Energy consumption per car-passenger-mile	2	1	4	8	5	7	9	6	3
Cold climate[a]	7	2	5	4	9	3	5	1	8
Size of house & percentage single family	1	1	6	6	8	5	4	3	8
Extractive industry GDP as percent of total GDP	2	1	n/a	4	6	n/a	3	5	7
Industrial GDP as percent of total GDP	7	8	2	1	6	4	5	9	3
Ratio of industrial energy consumption to industrial GDP	2	1	9	8	6	5	4	3	7
Degree of energy self-sufficiency	2	1	7	5	8	3	4	6	9
For reference:									
Energy/GDP ratio	2	1	9	6	7	3	4	5	8
Energy per capita	2	1	7	5	9	4	6	3	8
GDP per capita	1	3	4	5	9	6	8	2	7

NOTES: When a number is missing in rankings, it is due to a tie.
n/a = not available.
[a] Measured by degree days.
For a given factor, the lower the number, the greater the effect on raising the energy/GDP ratio.

Sources: J. Darmstadter, J. Dunkerley, and J. Alterman, *How Industrial Societies Use Energy: A Comparative Analysis* (Copyright © The Johns Hopkins University Press for Resources for the Future, 1977)
Based on data appearing in chapters 3 through 8 of this study, supplemented in the case of line 7 by information from United Nations, *Statistical Yearbook, 1974,* New York, 1975.

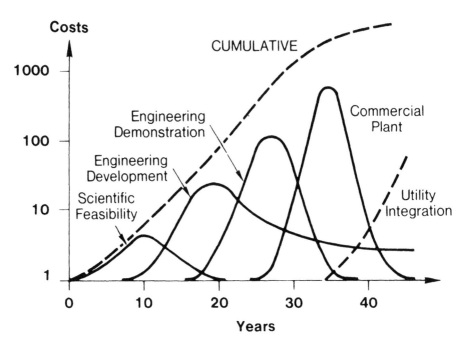

Figure 4   Phases of R&D

tive decisions or reduced investments. Here resistance to investments in new technology is proportional to the degree of uncertainty with respect to technology as it relates to operational characteristics, cost, demand, institutional parameters, and externalities, such as safety or pollution. (5)

Planning Philosophy

For any energy planning target, it is generally assumed that energy supply should be planned to just meet a projected energy demand. Unstated assumptions, such as this, can be extremely hazardous. Do we really want to plan our supply availability to equal a future energy demand? I think not, because an unanticipated deficit is too costly.

Figure 5 shows the additional annual social cost to the consumer of expanding electricity supply faster or slower than a projected growth in electricity demand. As indicated in this example, there is a highly asymmetric relationship between the social cost of an electricity capacity deficit and an electricity capacity surplus. The cost of the deficit results from the frequency of "blackouts", the loss of jobs, lower economic growth, and their consequences. Alternatively, the cost of a surplus is just equal to the calculable carrying charges of the capital investment. A capacity deficit is many times more costly than a capacity surplus of equal size. (6)

Economic Growth and the Quality of Life

The matter of economic growth really boils down to a decision on the part of society as to whether to sacrifice something useful and desirable right now so that people can be better off in the future. (7) For growth, the classical example found in the textbooks is that of using our labor and other resources to build durable goods (as opposed to consumer goods) like roads, subways, and dams that will be available for people not even born when those capital projects were initiated. Certainly, there are other ways in which the same choice can be made, e.g., the direction of intellectual resources to the invention of things like the generation of electricity from nuclear fusion that will also benefit future generations.

There are those who favor growth and those who do not. And the debate between these two groups has become fashionable over the past few years. (8) It would be presumptious on my part to try to reach a settled conclusion to the debate of whether continued economic growth is desirable, and whether it is possible. But there are some strong positive

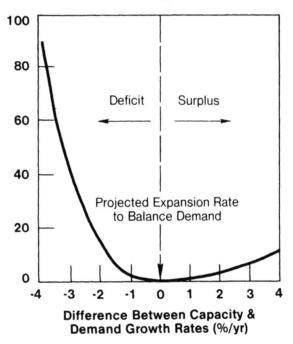

Figure 5   Social costs of supply-demand mismatch for electricity

Economic Growth and Conservation Technology 41

arguments being made for growth and its benefits, one of which is improvement in the quality of life.

For example, William Nordhaus and James Tobin have tested out the question of whether a proper accounting of national income statistics would show the supposed gains from economic growth to be non-existent.[9] The test required recalculating measured national income to account for disamenities of modern life. This was done by subtracting from income, government services (such as police and defense) which in less complicated times were largely unnecessary, and also by netting out the social costs of pollution. Urban crowding, crime and insecurity can be considered social costs of growth - hence the need to subtract a portion of income gains associated with urbanization. Nordhaus and Tobin used the wage differential between rural and urban areas as a measure of the disamenity.

After all of these recalculations and others on the same order, they found that what might be termed "clean" or "real" per capita income rose 42 percent between 1929 and 1965. This is as contrasted with the conventional 88 percent growth in per capita net national income. In other words, the benefits of growth in national income far outweigh the disamenities of modern life. All things considered, they concluded that growth has resulted in improvement in the quality of life for the average of the population.

Economic Growth and Technology

The past achievement of technology, the late Joseph Schumpeter was fond of saying, was that it brought the price of silk stockings within the reach of every shopgirl, as well as of a queen. The future promise of technology, he added, was like an "uncharted sea" where there was no reason to expect a slackening of the rate of output through the exhaustion of technological possibilities.[10]

In the quarter of a century since Schumpeter made those remarks, a number of economic studies have examined the technological component of economic growth.[11] The standard economic tool for such an examination is the Cobb-Douglas production function which relates economic output to capital, labor, and time (to incorporate technological change) and other factors. In its general form this production function has been represented as:

$$Y = e^{\lambda t} K^\alpha L^\beta ,$$

42   Chauncey Starr

in which Y is economic output, K is capital, and L is labor. λ, α, and β are constants. In this general form, assuming other things remain the same, output grows exponentially in time. This is representative of technological change. Based on this production function it is possible to maintain growth of output concurrent with reduction in resource consumption. This appears possible because under this representation of the production process, substitution of capital and technology for other resources is possible. However, this is only pragmatically valid under certain limited conditions, and the extent to which these factors can be substituted for one another has not been sufficiently explored.

In one controversial study,[12] employing American data for the period 1909-1949, Solow showed that the upward shift in the production function was at an annual rate of about one percent for the first half of the period and 2 percent for the last half. In addition, Solow concluded that gross output per man hour doubled over the interval, with seven-eighths of the increase attributable to technical change and the remaining one-eighth to increased use of capital. However, these important findings need careful interpretation.

First, although it is customary to measure and speak of the enhanced productivity of labor, this clearly is not the result of greater effort on the part of workers, or from more intensive conditions of sweat and strain, nor is there any indication that it came largely from more education, or from more initiative and incentives; nor, for that matter, from more energetic and clever executive management. Although such factors may play some role, the predominant explanation is technological improvement.

Second, it is artificial to separate capital formation and technology completely. New techniques do tend to be embodied in new kinds of equipment. It is possible to imagine a stationary state in which there is no net saving and investment, but in which there is considerable technical progress as the depreciation charges of worn-out equipment finance their replacement by technically better equipment. Still, no one will deny that innovations can be introduced faster in a society which is expanding its capital structure in addition to replacement. We all do learn from actually doing, and the society which gets to try out more new things will run that much ahead of the one which does little.

Without defining one parameter, or a group of parameters, as a measure of technological progress, it is possible to generalize from the evidence found in common growth from the various technical fields that technology exhibits an exponential growth pattern.[13] Although the techniques of technological forecasting can be quite complex, there are at least two predominant characteristics one can build forecasts on. First, when the technical parameter for a specific technique is plotted against time it follows a characteristic sigmoid curve of the form shown in Figure 6. Initially, the technique tends to experience a period of slow growth in its initial or conceptual phase, a subsequent period of exponential growth, and then a flattening as limiting factors are encountered, and the curve asymptotically approaches some upper value, which is definable when the limiting factor is known.

This initial phase of growth along a sigmoid curve can be expressed by the following infinite series:

$$\frac{\text{Output}}{\text{Limit}} = \frac{\varepsilon\,e^{at}}{1+\varepsilon e^{at}} \sim \varepsilon e^{at} - (\varepsilon e^{at})^2 + (\varepsilon e^{at})^3 - \ldots$$

Where, $\varepsilon e^{at} < 1$.

Because initial data in any gross situation supports the first term, the common projection is to neglect the higher terms and to extrapolate the first term until the "Doomsday" syndrome occurs.

Second, there is the common characteristic that the overall growth of a technological field is composed of a series of sigmoid curves where each specific technology contributes a small portion to the overall growth in end-use capability. This point is illustrated in Figure 7 to Figure 9 where the successive generations of technological steps have increased the performance of the power output of basic machines, and lighting efficiency as a function of time. The overall exponential growth rate can clearly be seen from these figures.

Although these figures are only representative of a much larger base, one needs only to turn to the technical publications and reports to have a glimpse at recent and pending technological advancements in the field of energy utilization. For example, a recent report of a NATO Science Committee Conference[14] highlighted energy problems and technological opportunities in heat, light, motion, electrolytic and electronic processes, residential and commercial systems, industrial systems, and urban systems, to provide energy for a growing society efficiently. One can be opti-

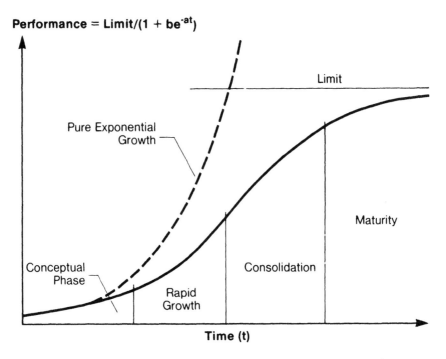

SOURCE: C. Starr and R. Rudman, "Parameters of Technological Growth," *Science*, Oct. 1973.

Figure 6   General form of the sigmoid curve

Economic Growth and Conservation Technology   45

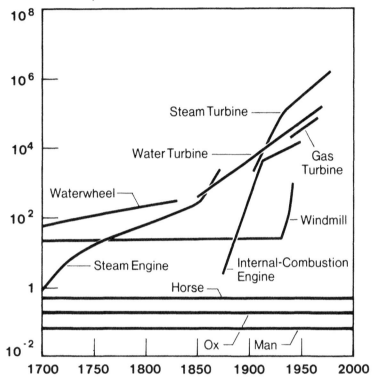

Figure 7   Output of power devices: 1700-2000

Source: Adapted from "Energy and Power"
          by Chauncey Starr. Copyright
          ©1971 by Scientific American,
          Inc. All rights reserved.

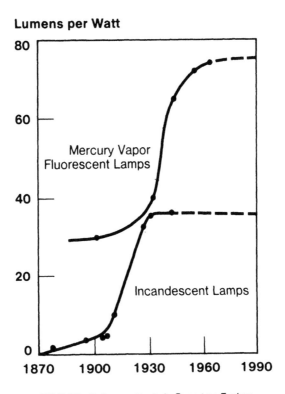

SOURCE: H. Darracott, et.al., *Report on Technological Forecasting*, 1967.

Figure 8   Illumination

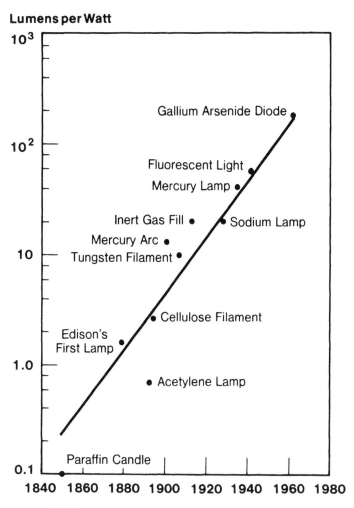

Figure 9   Illumination trends

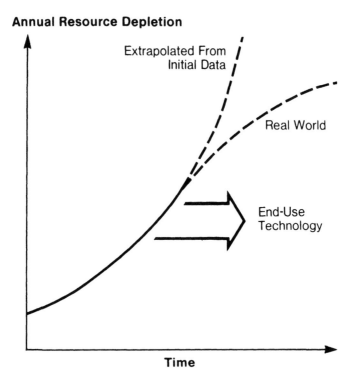

Figure 10 Annual resource depletion extrapolated from initial data and real world

Economic Growth and Conservation Technology   49

mistic that the anticipated technological advancements will
serve to significantly reduce future energy requirements and
also increase energy supply alternatives.

But could it not be expected that technology as a whole,
over the long-run, is approaching an inevitable inflection
point?[15]   I think not because we are so far from the the-
oretical limits of performance. Of course, it is impossible
to ascertain which portion of this aggregate technology curve
we are on, since overall technology development may also be
a sigmoid process. Intuitively, I believe, we are in the
growth phase, and if there are limits they lie far in the
future - perhaps at some time when societies reach a state
of omniscience, or when societies lose interest in the re-
investment process, or become nontechnical - like the
porpoise, intelligent but without machines. These future
states, however, seem quite remote.

Energy Conservation Technology

If we look at annual resource depletion over time, it
is clear that the rate of depletion has been exponential.
Figure 10 provides a hypothetical example of this trend. An
extrapolation from the historical data would suggest a continued exponential trend, but in the real world, we know that
individual resources become increasingly scarce eventually,
a limiting factor that causes our curve to asymptotically
approach some upper value. However, technological advancements in more efficient end-use over time have continued to
shift the resource depletion curve to the right and usually
forestall societies from reaching this limiting factor.

In addition, easily found and rich resources have low
costs. Alternatively, as these rich resources are "used"
up, low grade resources (which may be in larger pockets) are
exploited, but only at higher costs. This is shown in Figure
11, where curve A represents one energy form, say oil, and
curve B represents another energy form, say shale-oil. In
the static sense, as the cost of oil continues to rise, at
some point, the production of shale-oil should become attractive. But technological development of resource production
is likely to shift these curves to the left, so that an
alternative resource supply becomes economically exploitable
sooner, and at lower cost.

Technology has been an important key in shifting these
curves, Figure 10 and 11, so that industrialized societies
have not met with serious constraints, or shortages of energy.
And there is no reason or evidence to indicate that technological growth will stagnate, or that the system will be any

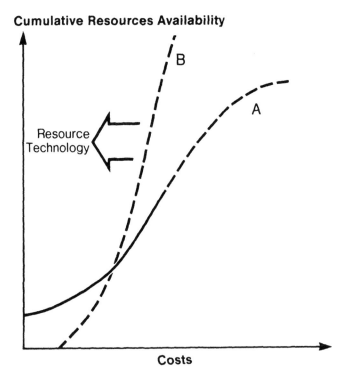

Figure 11 Resource availability and costs with shifts due to technology

Energy Availability

The prospect of an unlimited and economic energy resource has intrigued man's ingenuity for many years. As early as 1913, a steam engine was powered by a solar-heated boiler. Similarly, geothermal energy was considered as an inexhaustible energy resource since shortly after the advent of electricity itself. In 1904, the first geothermal plant was built at the Lardarello field in Italy. With the advent of an understanding of nuclear energy in the early 1940's, the fission breeder reactor was deemed as an almost unlimited supply. Fusion systems were conceived a decade later.

Today, all of these systems continue to be classified as advanced. Solar and geothermal electric systems are receiving substantial technical attention but, except for special cases, require major improvements to meet the competitive economic barriers.* Experimental breeder reactor systems have been operating for over ten years in the U.S., France, Great Britain, and the U.S.S.R. The 250-MWe Phenix reactor in France has been operating successfully for two years, and plans are underway there for a 1200-MWe reactor. These, also, need to establish their competitive economic positions, although they are well on the way to doing so.

The developing technology options which are currently receiving attention as future electricity sources are: fission breeder, geothermal, solar thermal conversion, photovoltaic conversion, biomass, nuclear fusion, wind, and ocean thermal gradients.

The principal incentive for investigating these options is that in each case the primary fuel cost is very low compared to anticipated fossil fuel prices. While these benefits may be offset by high capital costs, these systems could presumably provide protection against rapidly rising fuel prices or an unavailable supply, as has occurred with oil.

Certainly, the cost of producing electricity will be an important criterion before any operating system will con-

---

*The average annual investment projected for the next decade for electricity power expansion represents about 17 percent of all industrial investment of that period.(16) Thus any substantial increase due to use of non-competitive systems can have major national economic impact.

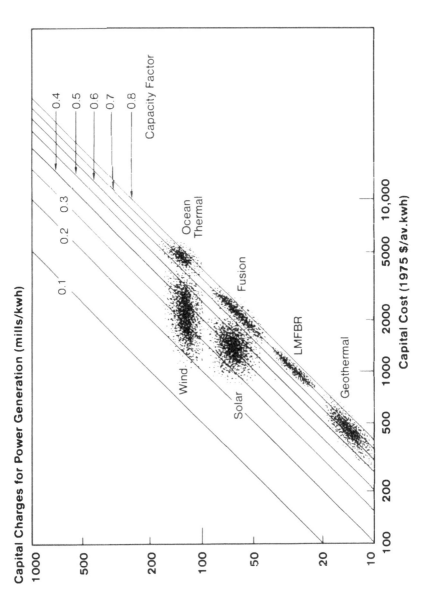

Figure 12   Estimated capital costs and capital charges for new electricity options

Economic Growth and Conservation Technology 53

sider undertaking the nationwide construction of a new type of plant, and the competitive costs of producing power by each of these options will greatly influence their chance for commercial success, and the usage integration rate should these systems become commercial.

The cost of electricity from these new power generation options is thus largely determined by plant capital costs and capacity factors.* Fuel makes at most a small impact in each case. The mix of capital and capacity factor is illustrated with optimistic projections of cost in Figure 12. Geothermal power from dry steam or hydrothermal reservoirs is the only one economically attractive today and is chiefly resource limited. The breeder is expected to be competitive when it is available. It is evident that the continuous availability of power is as important as the capital cost.

With respect to the other advanced options, <u>at present</u>: wind power appears to be economically attractive only for physically isolated small scale applications; power from ocean thermal gradients does not appear to be competitive under any foreseeable circumstance; fusion faces a host of scientific and engineering problems which must be solved before any meaningful appraisal of plant reliability, capital cost and system economics can be made; solar thermal electric, coupled with an energy storage system, if favored by substantial improvements in cost may possibly be considered by the year 2000 for intermediate load applications in areas of high solar insolation such as the Southwestern United States; and solar photovoltaic conversion will only be a significant source of energy in the twenty-first century if a fundamental technical breakthrough can lead to a low-cost and efficient solar cell. By the year 2000, this does not appear likely.

EPRI has evaluated the solar technologies through a comparison of the anticipated costs of these technologies with the projected costs of energy from other sources during the same time period. The parameter C_A/η_{PL} * I_{AV} crudely measures the target for economic competitiveness with displaced fuel: C_A being area related costs per area ($/m^2$), η_{PL} being overall plant efficiency, and I_{AV} being the annual average solar radiation collected per unit area (kW/m^2). The non-area related costs are roughly comparable to conventional system costs to which the solar options are being compared.

---

*Capacity factor is the fraction of the year that the plant produces full power equivalent.

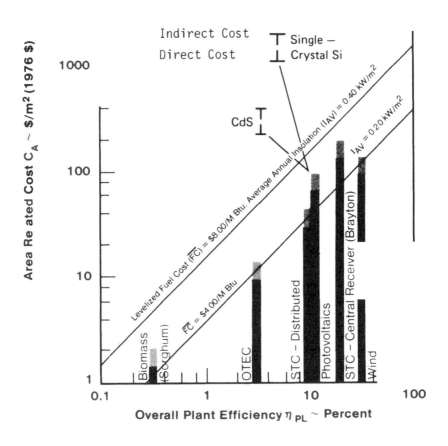

Figure 13 Allowable area related costs of alternative solar system concepts (1976 dollars)

Economic Growth and Conservation Technology 55

When all indirect and non-area related costs are included, the allowable area related costs (shown as a function of conversion efficiency) are as indicated in Figure 13. Also included in this figure are the current costs of many of these technologies. Note that the area related costs and efficiencies are on a log scale, so needed improvements in costs and efficiencies are quite significant.

Realistically, the nation should plan on satisfying no more than 2 percent of the year 2000 electricity demand with power from solar thermal electric and geothermal facilities. Perhaps an additional 2 percent could be supplied by the liquid metal fast breeder reactor if a national program for early commercialization of the breeder reactor is initiated in the near future.

These conclusions are in contradiction to those of the "selective optimists", i.e., individuals who firmly believe that, for example, the technological problems associated with solar, or ocean thermal electricity will be shortly solved, yet firmly believe that, for example, technologies for nuclear power waste storage are simply beyond our capabilities.[17] What this group is saying, is that they are sure that technology can solve all the problems which contribute to the goals they "selectively" choose to be desirable, but that technology cannot handle the problems for goals they perceive as undesirable. Such over-simplifications, if accepted as the basis for national policy carry the high risk of dangerously limiting future energy resource options.

Conclusions

In opting for economic growth, we are talking about future increases in the quality of life, improvements in the redistribution of income to overcome poverty, and maintaining full employment. It continues to appear that the benefits of growth far outweigh the disamenities of modern life. But economic growth with conservation hinges on the important parameter of growth in technology. Its potential depends on its actual application today and the likely applications tomorrow. Certainly, our conjecture about the future impacts of growth and conservation require an appreciation of the existing power and reach of modern science and some idea of the probable scientific developments in the future. From this we can speculate about the consequences on human lives. Certainly, the historical role of technology in stimulating growth cannot be denied. Such growth of technology has been exponential, and there is every indication that this trend will continue and will open new frontiers for social development in parallel with conservation of our resources.

56 *Chauncey Starr*

A vigorous approach to the development of all new supply technologies is required so that energy does not become a long-term constraint on economic growth and development. Nuclear power, including the breeder, must be pursued because it is now, and will be, an essential part of the total resources necessary to sustain an expanding economy. And other alternative sources such as solar, geothermal, biomass, tidal, oil shale, and synthetic fuels from coals should also be explored. For the future, all alternative energy sources should be developed so as to provide options for meeting future conditions, be they social, economic, or political.

References

(1) W. Hogan, et.al., "Energy and the Economy," (Energy Modeling Forum, Institute for Energy Studies, Stanford University, September 1977).

(2) C. Smith, ed., Efficient Electricity Use (Pergamon Press, New York, 1976, 2nd edition in press).

(3) C. Starr, "Energy Use: An Interregional Analysis with Implications for International Comparisons," Paper presented at International Energy Consumption Comparison Workshop, Brookings Institution, Washington, D.C. (September 1977).

(4) J. Darmstadter, J. Dunkerley, & J. Alterman, How Industrial Societies Use Energy A Comparative Analysis, (John Hopkins Univ. Press, Baltimore, 1977).

(5) J. Baer, et.al., "Government-Sponsored Demonstrations of New Technology," Science (May 1977).

(6) SRI, Decision Analysis of California Electrical Capacity Expansion (Stanford Research Institute Report, February 1977).

(7) R. Solow, "Is the End of the World at Hand?" Challenge (March/April 1977).

(8) E. Mishan, "Growth and Antigrowth: What are the Issues?" in The Economic Growth Controversy, (International Arts and Sciences Press, Inc., New York, 1976).

(9) W. Nordhaus, and J. Tobin, "Is Growth Obsolete?" in Economic Growth (NBER, Columbia University Press, New York, 1972).

Economic Growth and Conservation Technology   57

(10) J. Schumpeter, Capitalism, Socialism and Democracy, (Harper & Bros., New York, 1947).

(11) See, e.g., J. Kendrick, Postwar Productivity Trends in the United States, 1948-1969 (National Bureau of Economic Research, New York, 1973); R. Solow, "Investment in Technical Change," in Mathematical Models in the Social Sciences, ed. K. Arrow, et.al., (Stanford University Press, Stanford, 1959); E. Denison, Accounting for United States Economic Growth, 1929-1969 (The Brookings Institution, Washington, D.C. 1974).

(12) R. Solow, "Technical Change and the Aggregate Production Function," Review of Economics and Statistics (August 1957).

(13) C. Starr and R. Rudman, "Parameters of Technological Growth," Science (October 1973).

(14) E. Kovach, ed., "Technology of Efficient Energy Utilization," (Report of a NATO Science Committee Conference, 1973).

(15) D. Price, Little Science, Big Science, (Columbia University Press, New York, 1963).

(16) Bankers Trust Company, "Capital Resources for Energy Through the Year 1990", (New York, 1977).

(17) D. Hayes, Rays of Hope, (W.W. Norton & Co., New York, 1977).

3

Energy and Full Employment

W.W. Rostow

I

A Prima Facie Argument

Most policy-oriented analyses of the energy problem of the United States begin by assuming a national rate of real growth consistent with relatively full employment; calculate the energy requirements needed to sustain it, under stated assumptions about the potentialities for energy saving and policies to exploit those potentialities; and then proceed to estimates of the optimum mix of domestic energy production required to balance the growth-energy equation, at some viable level of oil and gas imports. President Carter's National Energy Plan (NEP), for example, assumed an annual average real rate of growth of GNP of about 4.3% between 1976 and 1985; proposed policies that would permit that growth rate to continue with an annual average increase of 2.25% in energy consumption, rather than the 3.0% otherwise assumed necessary; and then proceeded to the supply balance sheet and the policies believed necessary to generate the production and switch in energy sources that balance sheet demanded, if oil and gas imports were to be reduced by 1985 to about 6 mboed. The macroeconomic consequences of the plan, including its effects on investment,

---

I wish to thank Martin Baughman, Allen Davidson, William L. Fisher, J. Michael Gallagher, Charles Hitch, William Hogan, Milton Holloway, Irving Hoch, and William Miernyk for reading and commenting on this paper in an earlier draft.

60   W. W. Rostow

income, and employment, were dealt with in an extremely brief, fragmentary passage.[1] Its central theme was: "The macroeconomic impacts of the Plan would be quite small in a $2 trillion economy."[2]

That is also the central theme of the various longer term models designed to examine the effects of alternative energy policies on the real rate of growth over periods extending beyond 1985.[3]

I doubt that the macroeconomic consequences of a serious national energy plan will be "quite small." On the face of it, an effective national effort to contain oil imports at the level of, say, 6 mboed, when the present level is 9; when energy consumption is rising at 2-3% per annum and the decline in energy production is not yet reversed; when we must shift massively out of natural gas to coal, changing the locus of energy sources and the nation's transport requirements; when we must drill and find new oil and gas reserves at a rate sufficient to overcome a steady decline in production

---

1. Executive Office of the President, Energy Policy and Planning, *The National Energy Plan*, Washington, D. C.: GPO, April 29, 1977, pp. 97-98.

2. *Ibid.*, p. 97.

3. See, for example, Charles J. Hitch (ed.), *Modeling Energy Economy Interactions, Five Approaches*, Washington, D. C.: Resources for the Future, 1977, especially pp. iii-iv (Hitch) and Lester B. Lave's summation, pp. 278-300. Also, Energy Modeling Forum, Institute for Energy Studies, Report 1, Vol. 1, *Energy and the Economy*, Stanford, September 1977. For a lucid non-mathematical exposition of an energy-economy model, see Spurgeon M. Keeny, Jr. (Chairman), Report of the Nuclear Energy Policy Study Group, *Nuclear Power Issues and Choices*, Cambridge, Mass.: Ballinger Publishing Company, 1977, Chapter One, "Energy and the Economic Future," pp. 41-70. To a degree, the Energy Supply Planning Model developed by Bechtel National, Inc., is exempt from these criticisms. It traces back the investment requirements (including types of hardware and labor) of various energy targets and specifies their regional implications. It also embraces realistic time lags.

Energy and Full Employment   61

from old reserves (including Alaska) at a rate of about 5.5% per annum for oil, 7.5% for gas -- such an effort is bound to have large macroeconomic effects on the economy.

Quite aside from the massive investments required to damp the rate of increase in energy consumption, NEP calls for the development of 22.6 mboed in new domestic energy resources over the nine years between 1976 and 1985, if the declining trend in production from existing oil and gas fields is taken into account. This figure compares with the average for all 9-year periods since 1920 of 3.3 mboed.[4] The maximum increase for any 9-year period since 1920 was 9.0 mboed, over the years 1962-1970, during which the North Slope Alaska reserves were added to the nation's energy production capacity. As shall emerge, we are talking about an increase of 2-3 times in the relative flow of resources to a sector which, before 1974, normally absorbed about 15% of gross private domestic investment, say, 2.5% of GNP, and something like an average of 30% of total business plant and equipment investment (1947-1975). We are confronted, then, with the need for a massive as well as rapid change in the structure of the economy and the disposition of investment resources in a nine-year span; and, in addition, we must engage in substantial efforts (in research, development, and the early stages of commercial production) if, in fact, the post-1985 technologies (shale, synthetics, geothermal, etc.) are to play their predicted role in future energy supply.

Against that background of prima facie argument, this paper explores the following questions.

-- How would the aggregate performance of the economy as a whole be affected by a successful effort to achieve the approximate goals set out in the NEP?

-- How would the major regions be affected?

---

4. W. W. Rostow, W. L. Fisher, and H. H. Woodson, "National Energy Policy, September 1977, An Interim Overview," in *National Energy Policy: A Continuing Assessment*, Council on Energy Resources, University of Texas at Austin, January 1978.

62   *W. W. Rostow*

As always when relatively new questions are being posed, the data are not available in the form necessary to permit firm answers. But the systematic posing of these two questions and an effort to find approximate answers may be useful as a preliminary canvassing of a field about which, I believe, we are destined to learn a great deal more than we now know.

I shall proceed as follows:

-- First, evoke some historical evidence of shifts in the direction of investment, responding to a rise in the relative prices of one or more basic commodities, and briefly outline some of the consequences of such shifts.

-- Second, discuss the extent to which existing models attempting to relate the energy sector to the macro-performance of the economy are relevant to the two key questions posed.

-- Third, suggest by what routes the relative rise in the price of energy and expanded energy-related investment bear on the problem of achieving and maintaining a high sustained rate of growth and relatively full employment.

-- Finally, discuss some of the possible regional implications of the analysis as a whole.

II

The Effects of a Rise in Relative Price of a Major Basic Commodity: A Few Historical Illustrations

As I have argued at length and for a long time, the history of the world economy over the past two centuries has been marked by four irregular cycles in the relative prices of foodstuffs and raw materials. Since 1972 we have experienced the probable beginning of a fifth upswing.[5] The cyclical upswings were characterized by an overall inflationary trend (including money wages and interest rates); a relative shift of income to

---

5. The author's analyses of this problem are to be found mainly in *British Economy of the Nineteenth Century*, Oxford: At the Clarendon Press, 1948,

producers of foodstuffs and raw materials; deceleration or decline in real wages. In the downswings, the movements were, of course, obverse. The upswings began round about 1790, 1848, 1896, 1933, and 1972; the downswings, 1815, 1873, 1920, 1951.

For our limited purposes, the heart of the matter is the change in the direction of investment induced by these shifts in relative prices and, therefore, in profitability. Here, we are in a field where historical data are scarce, indeed. But a few examples where we have some statistical insight may be helpful in illuminating the process set in motion by the sustained rise in the relative price of a significant basic commodity.

In the first cycle (say, 1790-1848), there is considerable evidence that, responding to the course of agricultural prices, agricultural investment in Britain increased on the upswing, fell away relatively on the downswing. In the period 1788-1792, parliamentary acts of enclosure averaged annually 35; 114 for the peak period of agricultural prices (1808-1814); by the early 1840's the figure was 16.

Estimates of total agricultural investment are more difficult to establish. The best calculations we have exhibit a rise from £3.6 million c. 1790-1793; to £5.3 million c. 1815; a decline to £4.6 million c. 1830-1835.[6] Despite a sharp rise in the

---

Chapters I, III, IV, and VI, the latter three chapters originally published in the period 1938-40; *The Process of Economic Growth*, Oxford: At the Clarendon Press, 1953, 1960, Chapters 6, 8, and 9; A. D. Gayer et al., *Growth and Fluctuation of the British Economy, 1790-1850*, Oxford: At the Clarendon Press, 1953, 1975, Vol. II, Chapters IV and V; "Kondratieff, Schumpeter, and Kuznets: Trend Periods Revisited," *Journal of Economic History*, Vol. XXXV, No. 4, December 1975, pp. 719-53. Part Three of *The World Economy: History and Prospect*, Austin: University of Texas Press, 1978, traces out in detail the sequence of trend periods from 1790 to 1977.

6. The estimates are those of Sidney Pollard, reprinted in Francois Crouzet (ed.), *Capital*

64   W. W. Rostow

proportion of total investment in machinery over
these years, as one would expect in the decisive
initial phase of the industrial revolution (12.5%
c. 1790-1793 to 15.8% c. 1815 to 20.0% c. 1830-
1835), the proportion of agricultural to total investment roughly held its own in the upswing, but
fell away from 21.1% c. 1815 to 11.5% c. 1830-1835.

These shifts in the direction of investment
were, to a degree, made possible by a second effect
of the movement in relative prices; an income or
terms-of-trade effect. In the upswing, the judgment of historians is that British farmers were,
by and large, notably prosperous; in the downswing,
many were borne down by lower prices, although productivity improvements cushioned the position of
the more enterprising in the 1830's and 1840's.
This familiar generalization is hard to demonstrate
rigorously. For part of the upswing (1806-1815)
we have some fragmentary evidence as a result of
the wartime income tax. When the yield of that
tax, under its several schedules, is analyzed by
regions, the expansion of agricultural incomes
emerges clearly.[7] That expansion, in turn, permitted the increase in investment. Speaking of
agriculture, Hope-Jones concluded: "Under the
threat of war, food shortage and rising prices
'progress' became a patriotic duty and a profitable investment."[8] A good many new or expanded
country houses, as well as enclosed and well-
drained fields, flowed from this rise in income.
We lack equivalent evidence for the downswing, but
the complaints of the agricultural community and
pressures for tariff protection suggest that a
relative shift in income occurred, a trend validated by the rising trend in urban real wages.

Formation in the Industrial Revolution, London:
Methuen, 1972, p. 33. See, also, Phyllis Deane,
"Capital Formation in Britain before the Railway
Age," reprinted in *ibid.,* pp. 101-3, on agricul-
tural investment.

7. Arthur Hope-Jones, *Income Tax in the Napoleonic
Wars,* Cambridge: At the University Press, 1939,
Chapter VI, "The Yield on the War Income Tax,"
pp. 72-110.

8. *Ibid.,* p. 103.

And this shift in income distribution is undoubtedly related to the shift in the direction of British investment away from agriculture towards industry and (after 1830) the laying down of the highly productive British railway net.

Aspects of the American pre-1860 experience illustrate the same network of relationships. Although the role of industry increased over the period 1815-1860, the U. S. was still primarily an agricultural nation, its exports dominated by cotton, with wheat exports increasing its role in the fifteen years before the Civil War. The American terms of trade are, therefore, a fair reflection of movements in the relative prices of agricultural products and manufactures.

The terms of trade exhibit three intervals of increase: 1815-1817; 1828-1835; 1845-1851, although fluctuations persist at a high level until 1857.[9] For most of the 1820's and the first half of the 1840's, the terms of trade were, relatively, low.

The related shift in the direction of investment can be traced in two rough indicators: the purchase of federal lands and capital imports. Both exhibit high levels in the three periods of favorable terms of trade; both fall away in the 1820's and 1840's.[10] As one would expect, real wages rise in the 1840's, come under downward pressure in the 1850's.[11] This passage in American

---

9. Douglass C. North, *The Economic Growth of the United States, 1790-1860*, Englewood Cliffs, N. J.: Prentice-Hall, 1961, p. 244, charted on p. 93. It should be noted that the U. S. enjoyed an almost OPEC-like burst of prosperity in the 1790's when wartime price movements and transient status as an unchallenged neutral permitted the U. S. to exploit a doubling of its terms of trade from 1793 to 1799. See, also, Jeffrey G. Williamson, *American Growth and Balance of Payments, 1820-1913,* Chapel Hill: University of North Carolina Press, 1964.

10. Douglass C. North, *op.cit.*, pp. 244, 257 (southern land sales), and 259 (western land sales).

11. Alvin Hansen, "Factors Affecting the Trend in Real Wages," *American Economic Review,* March 1925,

66   W. W. Rostow

history introduces a further variable: immigration. The data, which begin at 1820, exhibit only a modest rise down to 1831; a sharp increase in the boom of the 1830's; a relative decline or deceleration down to 1845; movement to a peak in 1854. The annual average figure for 1840-1844 was 80 thousand; for 1850-1859, 384 thousand.

The case of Canada from 1896 to 1914 permits one to observe this mechanism at work, plus an additional potential dimension of the process. There is, as in the United States of the 1830's and 1850's, a shift in relative prices favorable to a producer of wheat and raw materials; a favorable movement of the terms of trade; a large influx of capital from abroad; and a massive increase in immigration.[12] The new dimension to be observed here is that the combination of forces at work in Canada in the two pre-1914 decades lifted that nation into its first sustained phase of modern industrialization.[13] Since 1868 a number of developments, including considerable railroadization and the expansion of processing industries, had prepared the way for the Canadian take-off. The point to be made here is that, when other conditions are propitious, an expansion of real income initiated by a favorable export price environment can have a significant expansionary effect on industry, over a wide front, as well as on the production of agricultural products and raw materials.

Vol. XV, p. 32.

12. See, for example, A. K. Cairncross, "Investment in Canada, 1900-1913," Chapter III in *Home and Foreign Investment, 1870-1913*, Cambridge: At the University Press, 1953, pp. 37-64. See, also, the author's *World Economy: History and Prospect*, Austin: University of Texas Press, 1978, pp. 171-172 and 449-450 where other sources are indicated.

13. In fact, the convergence between rapid industrialization and a boom centered on relatively high agricultural prices (favorable terms of trade, large capital imports, and immigration) occurred in the United States of the 1850's as well as during the pre-1914 generation in Russia (excepting immigration), Australia, and the São Paulo region of Brazil. See, for example, *The World Economy: History and Prospect*, pp. 427-30, 462-63, and 483-86.

Energy and Full Employment   67

What of the fate of capital exporters under these circumstances? Britain was the largest supplier of capital to pre-1914 Canada. In the long run, Britain benefited as the laying of the Canadian railway network to the wheat areas of Western Canada opened up a new and necessary supply of imported grain to supplant the attenuated supplies from the United States. While the Canadian boom was under way, British export industries gained, as did those in Britain deriving income from interest and profits. But the unfavorable shift in the British terms of trade, which, in effect, initiated the Canadian boom, was accentuated by the scale of the expansion in Canada and the concurrent expansions in Argentina and Australia. These were triggered by the same mechanism as that which set off the Canadian boom and were also sustained substantially by British capital exports. The result was downward pressure on British real wages and a lower level of domestic investment in Britain than would otherwise have occurred. In the period of high capital exports (1903-1913) gross domestic fixed capital formation in Britain fell from about 11% of GNP to 6-7%.[14] Net investment abroad rose from £43 million (1903) to £235 million; i.e., from 2% of GNP to 8.6%. Thus the proportion of total investment to GNP rose, despite the fall in domestic investment. Other decelerating forces were at work in the British and other advanced industrial economies of the time, but the scale of British capital exports rendered that deceleration more marked than in, say, Germany and the United States.[15]

One of the most dramatic reflections of the relation between a relative price movement and the pace of overall economic development is incorporated in the story of per capita income of the American South in relation to that of the rest of the country. Table 1 shows relative real income per capita for all the American regions from 1840 to

14. C. H. Feinstein, *Statistical Tables of National Income, Expenditure and Output of the U. K., 1855-1965*, Cambridge: At the University Press, 1976, pp. T48 (domestic investment) and T38 (foreign investment).

15. See *World Economy: History and Prospect*, pp. 174-194.

Table 1. Per Capita Income as Percent of U. S. Total, By Regions: 1840-1975

Year	USA	New England	Middle Atlantic	East North Central	West North Central	South Atlantic	East South Central	West South Central	Mountain	Pacific
1975	100	108	108	104	98	90	79	91	92	111
1970	100	108	113	105	95	86	74	85	90	110
1965	100	108	114	108	95	81	71	83	90	115
1960	100	109	116	107	93	77	67	83	95	118
1950	100	106	116	112	94	74	63	81	96	121
1940	100	121	124	112	84	69	55	70	92	138
1930	100	129	140	111	82	56	48	61	83	130
1920	100	124	134	108	87	59	52	72	100	135
1900	100	134	139	106	97	45	49	61	139	163
1880	100	141	141	102	90	45	51	70	168	204
1860	100	143	137	69	66	65	68	115	---	---
1840	100	132	136	67	75	70	73	144	---	---

Source: 1840-1970, *Historical Statistics of the United States, Colonial Times to 1970*, Washington, D. C.: Department of Commerce, 1975, p. 242; 1975, *Survey of Current Business*, Vol. 56, August 1976, Table 2, p. 17.

1975. Between 1840 and 1860 the cotton South experienced a decade of relative deceleration (1840-1850) followed by a decade of relatively high prices and prosperity. It lost, nevertheless, a little ground to the rapidly industrializing North. By 1880, however, the South's position had radically deteriorated. This was not merely the result of war destruction and Reconstruction but also of a decline of the cotton price from 43 cents per lb. in 1866 to 12 cents in 1880. The decline continued to a trough of 6 cents in 1898. This trend was accompanied by a global deceleration in the cotton textile industry and the volume of U. S. cotton exports. Thus, the value of U. S. cotton exports exceeded its 1866 level in only one year (1887) down to 1899. Meanwhile, industrialization in the South proceeded slowly, indeed. The relative lift in cotton prices reversed to a degree the relative income position of the South down to 1920: the cotton price was less than 7 cents per lb. in 1899; 13 cents in 1913; 34 cents in 1920. But, substantially influenced by the subsequent decline in cotton prices, the relative income position of the region sagged away in the 1920's and, of course, during the period of acute depression 1929-1933.

After 1933, once again the cotton price lifted; but this time the South, like Canada forty years earlier, was ready for sustained industrialization. With a large backlog of available technologies to apply, it moved forward over a wide front, gaining relatively on the more mature industrial states as it modernized its agriculture, developed an increasingly diversified industrial structure, and rapidly urbanized its social life. That process proceeded despite the relative setback to its basic commodity prices between 1951 and 1972. The relative upward shift in agricultural and energy prices since 1972 accelerated the narrowing of the income gap, as well as the flow of migrants to the South. The large flow of negroes to the northern cities began to reverse. No doubt, if we had such data, we would find that the flow of external capital to the South also accelerated.

The link of relative price to income movements is underlined by recent trends in population and relative income in the energy-rich states of the Mountain West and, of course, Alaska, as Table 6, below, suggests.

70   W. W. Rostow

As in the case of pre-1914 Britain, the states
of the Northeast and industrial Middle West lost
ground, relatively, at an accelerated rate since
the disproportionate rise in energy prices. The
number of manufacturing jobs declined absolutely
in the Northeast and industrial Middle West, unemployment was higher than the national average in
the recession of 1974-1975, remaining so in the
years of limited recovery, 1976-1977.[16] Lacking
internal balance of payments data for American
states and regions, we cannot measure the probable
increase in capital flows to the energy producing
states; but the movement of population to those
states has been impressive.

The reason for evoking these brief historical
illustrations is to suggest something of the dynamic process and its dimensions which a shift in
relative prices, of the kind we now confront in
energy, can set in motion. As among nations and
within nations, we confront not merely terms of
trade (or direct income) effects, but also changing
investment and population flows, triggering in some
cases far-ranging alterations in the pace and character of economic and social development. These
forces operate on both regions enjoying the advantage of high-priced basic commodities and those experiencing unfavorable terms of trade, from which
capital and population may flow.

III

Energy-Economy Models and the Energy Problem
of the United States

Against this background, we turn now to what
the energy-economy models tell us and fail to tell
us about the links of energy to the performance of
the economy.

They start with four empirical and, as nearly

---

16. For a more detailed analysis, see the author's
"A National Policy Towards Regional Change," *New
England Economic Indicators,* Boston: Federal Reserve Bank of Boston, May 1977, pp. 5-11. Also,
see Chapter 10 ("Regional Change: Conflict or Re-
conciliation") in the author's *Getting From Here
to There,* New York: McGraw-Hill, 1978.

as we know, correct assumptions.

       1. There is no foreseeable physical limit on the U. S. energy supply over, say, the next half-century; that is, coal, shale, and advanced forms of nuclear power could supplant the probable decline in oil, natural gas, and uranium reserves, even without large scale solar or fusion power.

       2. The marginal (and average) cost of energy will rise; that is, for some time we can expect the real cost of replacing a unit of energy consumed to exceed its present average price. We do not know with confidence what the rise in the real price of energy will prove to be.

       3. The total cost of energy in the U. S. economy as a proportion of GNP is relatively small; say, 5% in 1975. Therefore, even a quite substantial rise in the price of energy will yield only a modest damping in the rate of increase of real GNP, assuming GNP continues to rise regularly at rates not grossly dissimilar to those we have experienced since the end of the Second World War.

       4. We cannot estimate reliably, on the basis of past experience, what the price elasticity of demand for energy will prove to be in the face of a gross alteration of energy prices over a long period of time; nor can we estimate reliably long period changes in taste and in the income elasticity of demand for energy, as real income per capita rises; nor can we estimate reliably what the long-run elasticity of substitution of other factors of production for energy will prove to be. Therefore, in striking long-run demand-supply balances, considerable ranges are appropriate.

       With this framework of empirical assumptions, a good many energy-economy models have been developed and applied to long-run energy policy issues. They all derive, in one fashion or another, from the neo-classical growth models evolved over the past generation from the Harrod-Domar model.

       The neo-classical models have these basic characteristics shared by current energy-economy models.

       --Since both neo-classical and energy-economy models are, essentially, closed systems, the balance of payments and the level of energy imports are dealt with in casual *ad hoc* observations, if at all.

--Since these models are highly aggregated and closed system or national in their structure, neither differential regional effects within the United States nor the impact of U. S. energy performance on other regions of the world economy is dealt with systematically.

--They are long-run, full employment models, assuming either competitive market conditions or public policies which approximate such conditions.

--The rate of technological progress is exogenously determined, although some energy-economy analysts speculate, at least, on the damping effect of higher energy prices on the average rate of productivity increase.

--A stable consumption function is assumed, although some energy-economy analysts speculate, at least, about a possible rise in the proportion of energy-related investment required and a possible rise in the proportion of GNP invested if their growth and full employment assumptions are to be fulfilled.

--Since these models are long-term, the period of gestation of energy-related investment is not explicitly dealt with.

As always, then, we get out of models what we assume in the first place. The energy-economy models tell us that the U. S. commands the resource and probable technological capacity to weather, under the assumed conditions, a period of transition to higher cost energy sources with a relatively slight aggregate deceleration in GNP as compared to a situation where the real price of energy remained constant; that the potentialities of coal and shale give us considerable flexibility in exercising the nuclear option, and vice versa; and that the precise long run outcome will be affected significantly by what the various relevant elasticities prove to be.

If our central analytic task in the field of energy economics was to prove that a simple limits-to-growth view was incorrect, the energy-economy models might be judged helpful. By underlining that the United States, at least, commands the resources and technologies to meet its likely energy requirements over the long term, that the central problem is a rise in the real cost of energy, and that the low proportion of energy outlays to GNP makes that rise consistent with a continuing expansion in real per capita income, something useful might be accomplished for those who believe the contrary; although a good many advocates of the limits-to-growth view are unlikely to find the techniques of energy-economy models accessible or particularly persuasive.

On the other hand, the energy-economy models are substantially misleading both as an approximation to the energy problem confronted by the United States as of early 1978 and as a guide to current U. S. energy policy. In effect, these models wash out by assumption the critical features in our current situation.[17]

Specifically:

1. The peaking out of OPEC production capacity in the 1980's, perhaps as early as 1983, imposes a critical time constraint on U. S. energy policy, if the analyses of the CIA, MIT, and OECD experts are roughly correct, which I believe them to be (Chart 1). The crucial factors here are two: (a) the explicit decision of Saudi Arabia to expand production capacity slowly at a time when production capacity in some other substantial OPEC nations will begin to decline; (b) limitations on energy conservation which decree a quite substantial annual rate of growth of energy consumption if relatively full employment is to be sustained. The significance of the emergence of such an OPEC production capacity ceiling is heightened by the fact that Western Europe, taken as a whole, and Japan (as well as many developing countries) lack the potential alternative energy resources and technologies available to the United States. And,

---

17. The paper on *Energy and the Economy* of the Energy Modeling Forum, p. iv, is admirably explicit about the limitations of the conventional models.

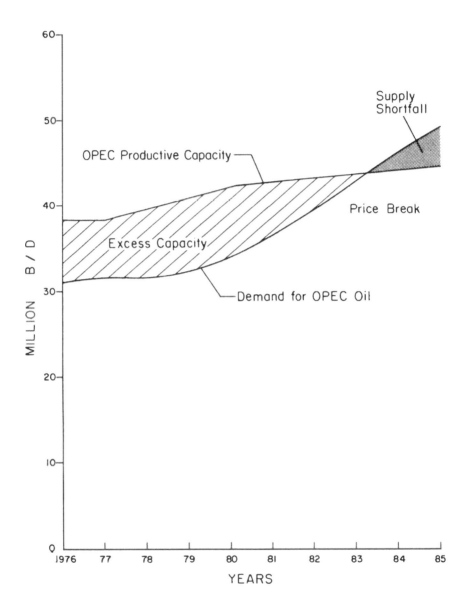

Chart 1. Projection of demand and capacity in OPEC production. Source: "The International Energy Situation: Outlook to 1985," Central Intelligence Agency, April 1977.

as in the United States, political forces are in-
hibiting the full exercise of the nuclear option.
It is not an exaggeration of current reality to describe the increasing dependence of the United
States, its allies, and others on a limited source
of external energy supply as the key economic and,
potentially, strategic fact on the world scene --
the latter proposition underlined by Secretary of
Defense Brown on October 26, 1977.[18] Even the
narrowly economic dimensions of this constraint are
not captured in current energy-economy models. The
pace at which the United States succeeds in reducing its energy imports will affect not merely the
possibility of sustaining relatively full employment and high steady growth in the OECD world, but
also the bargaining power of the importers vis-a-
vis OPEC and the real price of imported oil itself.
The implications of the required U. S. 1985 oil import level (up to 16 mboe), which will result from
the shortfall many analysts believe is implicit in
the implementing arrangements of the Carter Energy
Plan, are not dealt with in energy-economy models.
(See Table 2.)

        2. The real or believed differential im-
pact of energy policy on the various regions of the
United States has, almost certainly, been the
greatest political obstacle to the acceptance of
effective national courses of action with respect
to energy prices, the settlement of energy-environment trade-offs, and the government role in energy-
related investment. The energy-economy models
merely assume that, soon or late, these issues will
be resolved on optimum dynamic equilibrium terms.
The costs and consequences of a failure to achieve
such resolutions are not systematically explored
either for the aggregate performance of the economy
or the major regions.

        3. Similarly, the stubbornly high level
of unemployment in the OECD world since 1974 and
the slackened average growth rates, as compared to
the 1950's and 1960's, are neither noted nor explained in the energy-economy models. The failure
of public policy to permit or achieve by purposeful

---

18. Remarks prepared for delivery at the 25th an-
niversary meeting of the Council for Financial Aid
to Education, New York City (News Release,
Department of Defense, p. 3).

Table 2. VARIOUS 1985 PROJECTIONS OF DOMESTIC ENERGY PRODUCTION
AND SHORTFALLS RELATIVE TO NEP GOALS AND REQUIREMENTS
(All figures in millions of barrels per day in oil equivalents [mboed])

	COAL		OIL, GAS AND LIQUIDS		NUCLEAR		IMPORTS
	Projected Production	Shortfall	Projected Production	Shortfall	Projected Production	Shortfall	Projected
Congressional Research Service Library of Congress	Low 8.6	5.9	Most Likely		Low 3.0	0.8	Base Case 13.0
	Med 9.3	5.2	17.3	2.1	Base 3.8	0	Median or probable 15.9
	High 10.4	4.1					
Office of Technology Assessment, U. S. Congress	12.1	2.4	18.4 to 16.4	1.0 to 3.0	3.2	0.6	
U. T. Council on Energy Resources			Low 14.4	5.0			16.5
			Median 15.9	3.5			
			High 17.2	2.2			
General Accounting Office (excluding natural gas)							11.9-12.9
Independent Petrol Association of America			16.2	2.3			

Energy and Full Employment 77

action the energy prices the energy-economy models call for is, occasionally, noted; but the implications of that failure for levels of energy-related investment and employment are not explicitly explored.

4. The rising tendency in capital-output ratios (and declining per-hour increases in labor productivity) since the late 1960's in the OECD economies is neither examined nor explained, nor are the means to enlarge the proportion of GNP invested which some of these analyses require for long-run dynamic full employment equilibrium.

5. Finally, the dangers to the American and world economy implicit in the periods of gestation set out in Chart 2 are not considered. If the CIA analysis of the OPEC production capacity ceiling and its judgment about the level of global demand for OPEC oil are roughly correct, all but a few new sources of enlarged U. S. energy production (onshore and gulf oil and gas, surface coal mining on private lands) carry with them present periods of gestation too long to avoid a serious global supply restriction by 1983. Energy conservation lead times can also be quite long; for example, some seven years are required to turn over the existing stock of automobiles.

As presently formulated, then, the energy-economy models systematically fail to capture the major features of the energy problem confronted by the United States and the world economy -- now and over the decade or so ahead. George Santayana once observed:

> "There is a sort of poetic ineptitude
> in all human discourse when it tries to
> deal with natural and existing things.
> Practical men may not notice it, but in
> fact human discourse is intrinsically ad-
> dressed not to natural existing things
> but to ideal essences, poetic or logical
> terms which thought may define and play
> with. When fortune or necessity diverts
> our attention from this congenial ideal
> sport to crude facts and pressing issues,
> we turn our frail poetic ideas into sym-
> bols for those terrible irruptive things.
> In that paper money of our own stamping,

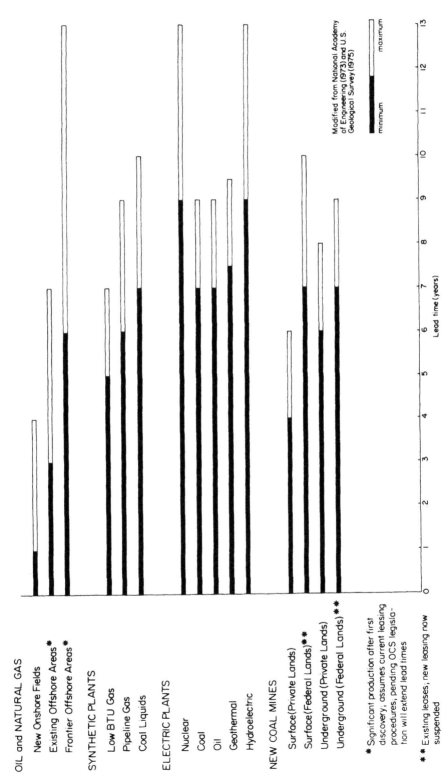

Chart 2. Lead times in domestic energy development.

Energy and Full Employment 79

the legal tender of the mind, we are
obliged to reckon all the movements
and values of the world."[19]

The "paper money of our own stamping," represented
by current energy-economy models, does not illumi-
nate the "crude facts and pressing issues" the
energy crisis inescapably imposes on us. These
models grip neither the urgency of the task, nor
its international and regional dimensions, nor its
linkage to the costly retardation of the American,
OECD, and non-OPEC developing economies since 1974.
As I wrote some years ago in another context:[20]

"It is an old story in the history of
economic thought that the variables assumed as fixed or given, for purposes of
formal exposition or convenience, tend
to disappear from consideration among
the objects of policy."

IV

Required Energy Investment and the
Return to Full Employment

In turning now to those "crude facts and
pressing issues," I shall not proceed by systematic
modification of one or another energy-economy model. I am inclined to believe that portions of the
argument that follows are capable of translation
into modified formal growth models.[21] And it
would, surely, be useful if some of the practition-
ers of the art would try to render their models
more realistic and relevant. But I shall here approach the problem through more conventional

19. George Santayana, *Character and Opinion in the
United States*, New York: Charles Scribner's Sons,
1920, pp. 167-168.

20. *The Process of Economic Growth*, Oxford: The
Clarendon Press, 1953, 1960, p. 90.

21. For an exercise in modeling not wholly irrele-
vant to the energy-economy problem, see W. W.
Rostow and Michael Kennedy with the assistance of
Faisal Nasr, "A Simple Model of the Kondratieff
Cycle," *Research in Economic History*, Spring/Summer
1979, Vol. 4, (forthcoming).

80 W. W. Rostow

economic analysis.

The argument can be summarized as follows: the relative stagnation of the OECD economies is the result of a failure of investment to revive to the extent that it did during the cyclical recoveries of the 1950's and 1960's; this failure is related to the impact on the rate of increase of real private income of the rise in energy prices; in the United States, at least, the order of magnitude of the energy-related investment required between now and 1985 to reduce U. S. oil imports to something like 6 mboed is sufficient to bring the American economy back to relatively full employment; the regional locus of this investment would be such as to mitigate some, at least, of the problems of the hard-pressed Northeast and industrial Middle West, as well as to accelerate the rapid expansions under way in the Mountain and West South Central states. The effect on the South Atlantic, East South Central, and Pacific Coast states (excepting Alaska), which have a stronger underlying momentum than the states of the industrial North, falls somewhere in between.

Chart 3 catches vividly the failure of investment in the six major OECD economies to recover from the recession of 1974-1975 with the resilience exhibited in previous cyclical expansions. This phenomenon stems from the anatomy of the great OECD boom of the previous two decades. In economic jargon, investment was driven forward in this period by the accelerator. The rapid increase in real income per capita, strengthened after 1951 by falling or relatively low prices for energy and other basic commodities, permitted the income elasticity of demand to express itself strongly in these directions: the further diffusion of the private automobile, durable consumers goods, the migration to suburbia, the expansion of higher education, medical services, and travel.[22] The rapid expansion of these sectors, in turn, stimulated investment over a wide front in North America, Western Europe, and Japan. Thus, it was the accelerator which lay at the basis of the great boom of the 1950's and 1960's in the OECD world:

---

22. For a detailed analysis in these terms, see *The World Economy: History and Prospect*, Part Three, pp. 247-286.

Energy and Full Employment   81

a powerful expansion of investment based on an expansion of real income sustained, in part, by falling or relatively low prices for basic commodities.

The radical upward shift in the prices of energy (and, to a degree, other basic commodities) after 1972 struck at the pillars of this majestic expansion in three ways. First, some of the leading sectors were energy-intensive and were affected by the price-elasticity of demand. Second, the expansion of real income was decelerated, as a matter of trend, by the unfavorable shift in the terms of trade for the OECD as a whole, despite the good fortune of Norway, now Britain, and the U. S. energy-producing states. Between 1972 and 1975, the price of agricultural exports in world trade rose by 83%, minerals (including fuels) by 213%, industrial products by 54%. The value of OPEC's exports rose from 6.6% of the world total to 13.4%.[23] Third, the slowness of the adjustment of public policy to the new trend period yielded an incomplete cyclical revival from the 1975 cyclical trough, which compounded the effect on the path of personal real income of the unfavorable shift in the terms of trade. Thus, we can observe what is now becoming chronic, substantial idle industrial capacity in the OECD world, notably acute in the steel industry.

It is not unfair, I believe, to characterize the plan of the Carter Administration to return to full employment as a kind of attempted replay of the great neo-Keynesian economic expansion of the Kennedy-Johnson years, this time without a large expansion in military expenditures but with what might be called a Ray Marshall addendum in the form of a substantial public services job program.

I am skeptical that it will work. I am skep-

---

23. See Hajo Hasenpflug and Mathias Lefeldt, "Structural Changes in World Trade since the Oil Crisis," *Intereconomics*, Hamburg, July/August 1977, pp. 187-191. A shift of this order of magnitude only occurred twice before in modern economic history: to Great Britain during the French Revolutionary and Napoleonic Wars when it dominated overseas trade; and to the United States as between the years immediately before the Second World War and those immediately afterward.

Chart 3. Cyclical Behavior of Non-Residential Investment in Seven Major Countries, 1955-1978

(Half years, volume indices, peak 100)

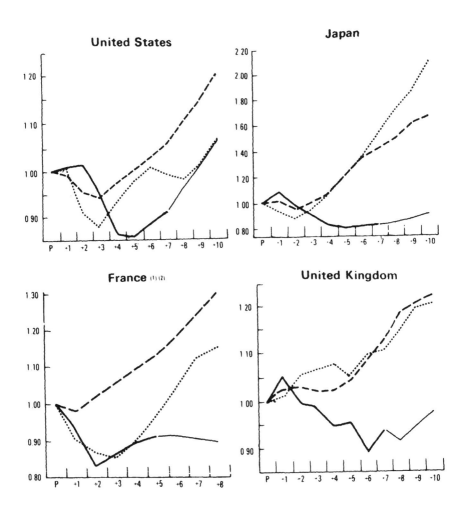

Chart 3. (continued)

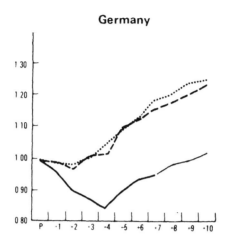

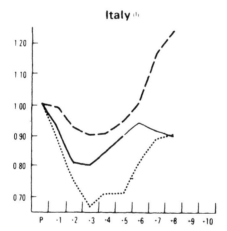

——— Present cycle, actual data
———— Present cycle, forecast
- - - - Average of previous cycles
..... Worst previous cycle

Note: The worst previous cycle is defined as the cycle with the deepest recession.

Source: *The OECD Observer*, July 1977, No. 87, p. 23.

84   W. W. Rostow

tical because this is not the early 1960's. At that time, energy, food, and raw material prices were relatively low. The real expenditures of consumers were rising rapidly -- at about 5% a year. Between 1971 and 1976 -- two comparable years in terms of the business cycle -- the rate was only 3.3%. The real outlays by consumers for energy-intensive automobiles and durable consumers goods rose at an annual rate of 10% between 1961 and 1965. The figure for 1971-76 was about 5%. Fixed investment in residential housing rose at an annual rate of over 5% in 1961-65; for 1971-76 the figure was minus 2%. In 1961-65 the total real government outlays for education, health, and other goods and services rose at an annual rate of 3.5%; for 1971-76 the figure was 1%. It was against this background that real private business investment rose at an annual rate of almost 10% in the first half of the 1960's, whereas it declined at an average rate of 0.6% between 1971 and 1976, despite some revival from the trough of the 1974-75 recession.

The conventional neo-Keynesian remedy for this situation would be expansionary fiscal and monetary policy. One can, of course, conceive of some increased level of consumers income, induced by extravagantly lowered taxes, extravagantly unbalanced federal budgets, and a rapid increase in the money supply that would permit automobile production and use, expanded sales of energy-intensive durable consumers goods, and a general overriding of high energy prices. Theoretically, incomes could be expanded enough for the income elasticity of demand to override to a considerable degree the price elasticity of demand for energy-intensive products. But retribution would certainly come in three forms: an accelerated increase in oil imports and severe balance of payments difficulties; accelerated inflation; and currencies gravely weakened on international exchanges, for floating exchange rates by no means wholly free domestic economic policy from external constraints as the experiences of pre-North Sea oil Britain and Italy suggest, as well as the current weakness of the U. S. dollar.

The alternative to a self-defeating conventional neo-Keynesian effort to expand effective demand is at once obvious and difficult.

It is obvious if one breaks out of neo-

Energy and Full Employment   85

Keynesian economics and asks the simple question: Where are the nation's great problems that require large investments? The answer is, surely, in these fields:

--energy production and conservation;

--water development, conservation, and transfer;

--investment in the transport system to deal with energy problems, to provide cost-effective urban mass transit systems (perhaps, simply, buses), and rehabilitate obsolescent parts of the transport network;

--land rehabilitation and forestry development (including development for biomass energy) and the modernization of rural regions of the South;

--the reduction of air and water pollution;

--and expanded research and development in energy and other resource fields.

The data are not now adequate for confident estimation of investment requirements in these fields. But from surveying the nation's authentic requirements in these fields with the data that can be mobilized, I, at least, emerge with considerable confidence that the means to full employment are at hand, if we address vigorously resource problems which will become progressively more serious with neglect.

Why, then, is the problem difficult? It is difficult for related intellectual and institutional reasons. Intellectually, our leading economists of what is sometimes called the mainstream, be they Republican or Democratic, are experts in manipulating effective demand. Children or grandchildren of John Maynard Keynes, they are awkward in handling the kind of resource and supply problems which have marched to the center of the stage so disconcertingly in the 1970's, but which have no formal place in neo-Keynesian models. Institutionally, we do not yet have the tools to mount large investment programs in these resource fields. We know how to raise or lower the Federal Reserve discount

Table 3. Gross Private Domestic Investment As a Proportion of GNP: Selected Years

(in 1972 dollars)

| | Total | | Gross Private Domestic Investment | |
		Fixed	Non-Residential	Residential
1952	13.9%	13.2%	8.9%	4.5%
1956	15.4	14.5	9.7	4.8
1965	16.2	15.0	10.3	4.7
1968	15.2	14.3	10.3	4.1
1972	16.1	15.3	10.0	5.3
1973	16.8	15.4	10.6	4.8
1974	15.0	14.3	10.6	3.7
1975	11.6	12.6	9.3	3.2
1976	13.6	12.9	9.1	3.7
3d Qtr 1977	14.8	13.7	9.4	4.3
Shortfall:				
1973-1977	2.0%	1.7%	1.2%	0.5%

Source: Bureau of Economic Analysis, Department of Commerce, *Business Conditions Digest*, various issues.

Energy and Full Employment 87

rate and the rate of expansion of the money supply.
We know how to enlarge or diminish the Federal budget deficit. Since the 1930's, we have learned how
to carry out public service job programs. But we
lack the institutions for mounting the kind of public-private sector collaboration required to increase investment in some of the necessary directions; and, with respect to the conventional
sources of energy and energy conservation, the democratic process in the United States has been unable to fulfill the price assumptions underlying
energy-economy models or settle firmly the energy-
environmental trade-offs.

In broad terms, the expansion of investment in
the directions listed above should constitute, in
the generation ahead, the equivalent, say, of the
opening up of the American West in the third quarter of the nineteenth century, the development of
the resources of Canada, Australia, Argentina, and
the Ukraine, in the two decades before 1914. We
would be evoking the multiplier as the catalytic
instrument to move us back to full employment to
supplant a weakened accelerator.

For present purposes, the narrower question
then arises: to what extent can we measure, even
roughly, the extent to which an effective national
energy program would close the gap in investment
which now prevents in the United States a return to
sustained full employment?

The gap on which we are focusing emerges from
Table 3.

It would be misleading to draw fine-grained
conclusions from the numbers in Table 3. Evidently, the role of annual inventory fluctuations has
affected the varying gap between total and fixed
private domestic investment. Residential investment has fluctuated over a considerable range, even
putting aside the post-1972 years. Perhaps the
best way to approximate roughly the investment
shortfall, as it bears on full employment, is to
put inventory fluctuations aside and compare the
proportion of fixed private investment at the 1973
peak with that in the second quarter of 1977. The
shortfall is 1.7% of GNP, roundly, $32 billion
(1977). Depending on the multiplier chosen, an

expansion of investment of that order of magnitude would go a considerable distance towards closing the full employment GNP gap now estimated in the range of $100-120 billion. If the multiplier were 2, two-thirds or half of the full employment gap would be covered.

Taking the arbitrary figure of 1.7% of GNP as a benchmark, the next question is whether a successful effort to fulfill something like the targets of the NEP would enlarge energy-related investment on a scale capable of closing that gap, assuming that gap is a structural phenomenon which will persist if not corrected.

There have been a good many estimates made of energy investment requirements for both production and conservation since 1974. They were made for different time periods and under varying assumptions. They are well summarized in *National Energy Outlook, 1976.*[24] But, certainly, the first recommendation I would make is that some branch of the federal government decide on a standard definition of energy-related investment; recalculate historical data in terms of that definition, both nationally and regionally; and publish regularly current estimates disaggregated by various types of energy production and conservation. Evidently, such data are highly relevant to the macro-performance of the U. S. economy and regional paths of development, as well as to the energy situation and its evolution. As shall emerge, the prospects are for energy-related investment to approximate in the decade ahead at least the proportion of GNP now allocated to residential housing construction, an item sedulously followed by macro-economists and prognosticators. It is a category which should certainly be of regular interest and concern to the Council of Economic Advisers.

Despite varying definitions (and occasional vagueness in specifying them), a rough consensus

---

24. Federal Energy Administration, Washington, D. C.: G.P.O., pp. 43-44 and 293-323. See, also, the array of estimates presented in J. Michael Gallagher and Ralph G. J. Zimmermann, *Capital, Manpower, Materials and Equipment Requirements for a Department of Commerce Projection*, San Francisco: Bechtel Corporation, December 1976, pp. 3-7.

Energy and Full Employment   89

is that to reduce U. S. oil imports to something
like 6 mboed by 1985, outlays of the order of some
7-800 billion in 1976 dollars will be required between 1977 and 1985. As we shall see, estimates
with broader definitions yield figures up to 60%
higher for energy-related investment down to 1985.

Table 4 presents one such estimate falling at
the lower end of the conventional range. It approximates, for example, FEA's estimate for the ten
year period up to 1985 when the latter is converted
into 1976 prices and reduced to a nine-year basis.
The FEA figure comes to $792 billion, also includ-
ing some downstream expenditures.

Table 4. U. S. Energy Investment, 1977-1985,
to Fulfill 1985 NEP Targets
(in billions of 1976 dollars)

	1977	1985	1977-1985
Oil and gas	19.6[a]	52.4[a]	304[a]
Electric utilities	24.8	33.0	230
Coal	2.9	4.6	35
Residential conversion)	)		(46
)	18.5	26.5 201	(
Industrial/ Commercial conservation)	)		(155
Total	65.8	116.5	770

a. Includes downstream expenditures of $6.5
billion in 1977; 9.3 in 1985; 70 for the
period 1977-1985.

Source: Allen Davidson and Martin Baughman, "Regional Patterns of Energy Investment, 1977 to
1985," in *National Energy Policy: A Continuing
Assessment,* Council on Energy Resources, University
of Texas at Austin, January 1978, pp. 182-211,
where sources and methods are indicated.

Davidson and Baughman calculated their investment
figure for conservation for 1977 by first approxi-
mating a figure for the whole period 1977-1985 and
then arbitrarily assuming a 4% per annum expansion

rate over the nine-year span. It is virtually certain that the 1977 figure ($18.5 billion for both household and business conservation investment) is somewhat too high, and that the growth rate required to achieve the conservation investment target will have to be higher than 4%. But one simple conclusion emerges from Table 4 and, indeed, from all other such calculations; namely, that if the United States deals seriously with its energy problem, energy-related investment will constitute a leading growth sector over the next decade and, almost certainly, beyond. The point can be made most simply by comparing the annual average rate of growth of energy investment in Table 4 (7.4%) with the assumed real rate of growth of GNP (4.3%).

The question then arises: Is the energy sectoral complex a sufficiently large part of the economy so that its expansion at some such rate would narrow significantly the current investment gap?

As of 1974, investment outlays for energy production, as estimated by FEA, were $37.74 billion in current dollars.* This sum constituted about 2.7% of GNP; 17.6% of gross private domestic investment; 25.3% of fixed non-residential investment; 33.3% of business expenditures for new plant and equipment.

The equivalent figures for the second quarter of 1977 are, of course, more uncertain. Now including a component for energy conservation (perhaps exaggerated in Table 4), they may approximate 3.0% of GNP; 19.2% of gross private domestic investment; 30% of fixed non-residential investment.

If an average 4.3% real growth rate is maintained down to 1985 and if the fixed investment proportion rises back to its 1973 level of 15.4%,

---

*This figure has been subsequently revised by the Department of Energy to $37.98 billion. The figure for 1975, the last year for which official estimates now exist, is $39.16 billion. This constituted about 2.6% of GNP; 21.3% of gross private domestic investment; 22.6% of fixed non-residential investment; 34.7% of business expenditures for new plant and equipment.

1985 energy-related investment would constitute 4.7% of GNP, 30.6% of gross fixed private domestic investment. As compared to our 1.7% of GNP investment shortfall, energy-related investment would have increased by 2% of GNP as compared to 1974, 1.7% as compared to 1977.

Roughly speaking, then, conventional plant and equipment estimates of the necessary increase in energy-related investment involve something just short of a doubling of its proportion to GNP by 1985, as compared to, say, 1974; and the enlargement covers a significant proportion of the current full employment investment gap, depending on the multiplier and the size of the gap assumed.

Table 5 presents energy investment estimates in the higher range. For purposes of easy comparison, the Davidson-Baughman estimates in Table 4 are repeated.

The totals in Table 5 would require a rise in the average proportion of energy-related investment to total fixed investment, over the period 1977-1985, of between 29.2% and 40.5%, assuming that the 1973 rate of 15.4% of GNP is re-established.[25] These estimates suggest energy-related investment would average over the period somewhere in the range between 4.4% and 6.1% of GNP. If we take the average within these ranges (5.25%) we are talking about approximately a doubling in the proportion of energy-related investment to total investment and GNP over the whole period 1977-1985 as opposed to the situation in 1974.

For our limited purposes, it is not necessary to isolate precisely the differences between the estimates in Tables 4 and 5. Evidently, Table 5 includes a considerably higher figure for utilities (conversion plus nuclear), as well as a significant item for synthetic fuels, shale, etc. and the cost

---

25. Since the Kozmetsky-Konecci calculations are estimates for the whole period 1977-1985, they lend themselves only to average investment rates. The proportions in the text are, therefore, not comparable to those above on pp. 22-24 for the years 1977 and 1985.

Table 5. Estimated Energy Investment, 1977-1985
to Fulfill 1985 NEP Targets

(in billions of 1976 dollars)

		Low	High	Davidson-Baughman Estimate
A.	Conservation Program			
1.	Residential Insulation	53	147	(46
2.	Residential Solar	5	15	(
3.	Industrial/Commercial Insulation	125	200	155
4.	Transportation - Auto/Truck/Bus	?	?	--
5.	Federal Insulation Program	2	2	--
	Sub-total	185	364	201
B.	Energy Supply Investments			
6.	Oil and Gas	250	320	304
7.	Federal Strategic Reserve - Oil	6	8	--
8.	Utilities Industry - Conversion	240	250	230*
9.	Coal	36	49	35
10.	Nuclear Power	108	143	--
11.	Synthetic Fuels, Shale & Other	10	25	--
	Sub-total	650	795	569
	Grand Total	835	1159	770

* Including nuclear.

Source: George Kozmetsky and Eugene B. Konecci, "National Energy Plan and Investment Analyses," in *Preliminary Assessment of the President's National Energy Plan,* Council on Energy Resources, University of Texas at Austin, May 11, 1977, p. 354, where sources and methods are described.

Energy and Full Employment   93

of the strategic reserve. It also includes rough
first approximations for infrastructure outlays by
state and local governments, the building industry,
and transport required in direct support of energy-
related investment calculated conventionally as
plant and equipment. In the case of coal, for example, this procedure increases the range of required investment from $24-30 billion (1976), for
plant and equipment, to $36-49 billion. Whatever
the precision of the figures, conceptually energy-
related investment should include such direct-
support infrastructure outlays.

Whatever the imperfection of these pioneering
calculations in a somewhat new and uncertain field,
it is palpable that the necessary rise in energy-
related investment down to 1985 is of an order of
magnitude sufficient to close or exceed the investment shortfall in the U. S. economy as of 1977.
To put the order of magnitude we are examining into
perspective, it may be useful to recall that in the
great boom of the 1850's gross railroad investment
accounted for about 15% of gross capital formation
reaching almost a fourth at the peak in 1854. The
gross investment rate in these years may have ap-
proximated 18%, so that railroad investment averaged about 2.7% of GNP, reaching 4.5% at the 1854
peak. During the years 1870-1895, the railroads
accounted for something like 13% of aggregate gross
investment, about 1.7% of GNP, with a peak in the
early 1870's of perhaps 5.75% of GNP. To cut U. S.
oil imports back to about 6 mboed by 1985 may prove
to be, proportionately, a bigger effort than the
railroadization of the American West.

The order of magnitude of increased energy
investment requirements, when measured in some such
way, has, in various analyses, led to the question
of a possible capital shortage; that is, demands
for capital which cannot be met from current savings rates at relatively full employment.

In terms of the argument thus far developed
here, the capital shortage issue might be put as
follows: What problems are posed for the execution
of an effective national energy plan if, in fact,
the private investment gap of 1974-1977 disap-
peared, on its own, without radically increased energy investment; or (which is quite possible)

rising investment requirements for transport, water development, pollution control, raw materials, and in other resource-related fields yield total capital requirements which, along with those for energy, bring about the need for investment priorities if acute demand-pull inflation is to be avoided?

In terms of method, the most satisfactory treatment of this problem is that of Bosworth, Duesenberry, and Carron.[26] They ask, in effect, if an assumed shift in the proportion of energy investment from 24.6% in 1973 to 32.6% in 1980 can be accommodated without a capital shortage or an increase in the proportion of GNP invested. Their answer, as of the time of their study, was that only a slight increase in the overall investment proportion would be required if the following major conditions were fulfilled:

--the economy resumed promptly its full employment path;

--the proportion of resources absorbed in residential investment, the interstate highway system and education declined;

--the federal government generated a budget surplus;

--there were no new starts in social programs.

To approach rationally the possible priority problem we shall face, evidently we need sectoral investment-requirement estimates in a number of resource fields, aside from energy. My own best guess is that, if the energy, water, transport, and other resource-related problems, where degeneration is now under way, were to be successfully confronted by the United States, our problem would, indeed, become one of priorities, and the unemployment problem as we have known it since 1974-1975 would disappear. For an economic historian, this conclusion is no surprise. By and large the other four periods of sustained relatively high prices

---

26. Barry Bosworth, James S. Duesenberry, and Andrew S. Carron, *Capital Needs in the Seventies*, Washington, D. C.: The Brookings Institution, 1975.

for basic commodities have also been periods of relatively low unemployment.

V

Energy Investment: The Impact on the Regions

We turn now to an area where data and analysis are even less well formulated than in the case of energy-investment requirements; that is, the regional impact of a successful effort to approximate the NEP targets. I shall set aside the direct income-transfer effects of the array of taxes and rebates proposed to the Congress by the Carter Administration; for their fate is still undecided as this paper is written. I shall concentrate on attempting to sketch the possible rough directions of change under the headings set out in Part II; that is, effects on income, investment, population movements, and industrial structure.

It may be, first, useful to give some quantitative form to a fact of which we are all instinctively aware; namely, that growth rates have varied widely in the various regions over recent years. As noted earlier (pp. 9-12), the normal catching-up process of the South and Southwest since the 1930's was accelerated by the relative price movements since the close of 1972. The result is seen in Table 6 which exhibits the average annual increase in real earnings for the period 1971-1976 and population change by regions.

Data do not permit calculations of gross state or gross regional income; but changes in real earnings are a reasonable surrogate, although the national rate of increase in real earnings from 1971 to 1976 was slightly less (2.4%) than for real GNP (2.7%).

In a large continental economy one would not expect uniform regional growth rates. But a spread of regional real income growth rates over a range of almost 9 to 1 is an impressive phenomenon. It underlines the inadequacy of national macro-data, macro-modeling, and macro-policy. With respect to population, the United States contains regions with virtually stagnant populations, others with popula-

W. W. Rostow

Table 6. Annual Average Percentage Growth
in Real Earnings by Regions: 1971-1976;
Percentage Population Change Between
1970 and 1975

(Calculated from data in 1972 dollars)

	Real Earnings Annual Average Change	Population	
		Total Change 1970-1975	Annual Average Change
New England	.94%	2.9%	0.57%
Mid-Atlantic	.60	.1	0.03
East North Central	1.84	1.8	0.35
West North Central	2.20	2.2	0.44
Southeast	3.65	9.9	1.67
Southwest	5.26	7.9	1.54
Mountain	5.05	16.4	3.08
Pacific	3.14	6.2	1.20
(Alaska	23.81)	---	----
U. S. National Average	2.415	4.8	0.94

Source: Growth in real earnings from data calculated by Daniel Garnick, Bureau of Economic Analysis,
Department of Commerce; population change, Bureau
of the Census.

lations expanding as fast or faster than those in
developing nations.

For our purposes, these data underline the
prima facie case for linking energy to growth.
Putting aside the vertiginous figure for Alaska,
the highest growth rates are in the two regions
containing large energy resources exploitable at
current prices: the Southwest and Rocky Mountain
states. Although here placed in the Southeast,
Louisiana enjoyed a rise of 4.71% in real earnings.
The figure for Wyoming (8.84%) is the highest for
any state except Alaska.

The rise of real income in these states is,
of course, compounded of the three related elements
delineated in Part II of this paper: the terms of

trade (or income) effect; population expansion; and increased investment. I, at least, do not command the data to decompose these elements and assign them relative weights; although their analytic interconnection should be underlined.[27]

Before turning to estimates of approximate regional distribution of energy-related investment, in an effective national energy program, it is worth underling a few general propositions.

First, of course, there is, despite the strong forces at work in the various regions, a complex set of interconnections within the national economy. Rapid expansion or deceleration in one region affects all the others. A general cyclical expansion or recession in the national economy leaves its mark, in different degree, on all the regions. A weakening or strengthening of the dollar alters import prices throughout the economy.

Second, so far as energy is concerned, the greatest stake is one that is universally shared by all the regions; namely, that a reduction in U. S. oil imports permits the OECD world (including the U. S.) and the developing countries which import oil to experience low levels of unemployment and rapid growth. A period of international and domestic energy rationing (or a brutal struggle for scarce supplies) is likely to be a time of extreme tension and frustration. Moreover, it is

---

27. The best analyses of regional shifts combining income, population, and structural change are those of William H. Miernyk; for example, "Regional Shifts in Economic Base and Structure in the United States since 1940," paper prepared for the Conference on a National Policy Towards Regional Change, Alternatives to Confrontation, University of Texas at Austin, September 24-25, 1977. For a thoughtful preliminary exploration of energy in relation to this process, see Irving Hoch, "The Role of Energy in the Regional Distribution of Economic Activity," a paper prepared for the same conference. Among the many studies of recent population movements, including the astonishing movement away from metropolitan areas, see Peter A. Morrison, "Current Demographic Change in Regions of the United States," also prepared for the Austin regional conference.

98   W. W. Rostow

a phase which would, almost certainly, see a marked further rise in international oil prices, as the CIA has predicted. In short, there is a large negative interest in avoiding a global energy crisis in the 1980's shared by all the American regions.[28]

Third, a successful effort to conserve and to expand production sufficiently to reduce imports sharply by 1985 would have the general effect of assuring energy supplies throughout the country, including the energy-importing states and regions. There is evidence that the believed unreliability of energy supplies is one (among other) reason for the shift of manufacturing capacity towards energy-producing states.

Nevertheless, as Table 7 indicates, quite distinctive regional effects are likely to flow from an effective national energy production plan.

The total energy production investment figure for the UT model was built up mainly from regional estimates; the Bechtel estimate is the FEA Reference Case, 1976-1985, reduced to a nine-year basis. Both estimates are, essentially, for construction costs, excluding interest during construction, lease costs, operating capital, etc., which, the Bechtel analysts estimate, could add about 35% to their figure.

To some extent the differences as between the two production investment estimates stem from differing assumptions about the energy production mix over the next decade.

The difference in assumed oil and gas drilling costs almost certainly explains, for example, the difference in the investment figure for the West South Central region in Table 7. The higher electric utilities figure in the Bechtel estimate (since reduced), as well as its figure for coal

---

28. For further vivid expositions of the dangers to the American economy implicit in this situation, see Charles Schultze, Remarks before the American Council of Life Insurance Annual Meeting, New York, November 30, 1977; and Richard N. Cooper, a speech before the Annual Business Forecasting Conference at the University of California, Los Angeles, December 8, 1977.

Table 7. Energy Production Capital Requirements by Regions to 1985: Nine Years

(billions of 1976 dollars)

	UT Estimate	%	Bechtel Estimate	%
New England	6.8	1.4	13.5	2.5
Middle Atlantic	31.9	6.4	56.2	10.6
South Atlantic	48.0	9.6	54.9	10.3
East North Central	44.8	9.0	77.0	14.5
East South Central	44.4	8.9	45.5	8.5
West North Central	37.6	7.5	38.8	7.3
West South Central	155.9	31.3	125.4	23.6
Mountain	76.6	15.4	42.9	8.1
Pacific	52.2	10.5	77.6	14.6
	498.2	100.0%	531.8	100.0%

Sources: The "UT Estimate" was calculated by Allen Davidson and Martin L. Baughman, *op.cit.* The "Bechtel Estimate" is that of J. Michael Gallagher and Ralph G. J. Zimmermann in *Regional Requirements of Capital, Manpower, Materials, and Equipment for Selected Energy Futures,* San Francisco: Bechtel Corporation, November 1976. The regional breakdowns have, in this comparative table, been reconciled; and the Bechtel estimate converted from third quarter 1974 to 1976 dollars (using the deflator for fixed private non-residential investment) and from a ten to nine-year basis.

---

synthetics and shale, would also alter the regional investment proportions.

Turning to conservation, the FEA estimated that energy-conservation investment would add about $250 billion (1975) to energy-related capital outlays, which converts to $236 billion (when converted into 1976 dollars and put on a nine- rather than ten-year basis.[29] The Bechtel estimate does

---

29. FEA, *National Energy Outlook, 1976,* Washington, D. C.: G.P.O., p. 43.

Table 8. Energy Production Capital Requirements by Sector to 1985: Nine Years

(billions of 1976 dollars)

	UT Estimate	Bechtel Estimate
Electric Utilities (including nuclear)	230.25	275
Oil and Gas	230.60	210
Coal	35.17	42
Coal Synthetics and Shale	---	5

not include conservation investment. The UT analysts did attempt a regional breakdown of a somewhat lesser total ($201 billion) by proportioning residential conservation investment by number of households, commercial-industrial conservation investment, by value added in manufacturing (1972). The results are set out in Table 9.

Total energy-related investment (production plus conservation) by regions, per household, and per dollar-value added in manufacturing are given in Table 10.

With these rough data in hand, two broad conclusions can be drawn about the regional impact of a successful NEP.

First, energy conservation investment emerges as a major category, of the same order of magnitude as investment in utilities (including nuclear) and oil and gas. Moreover, its regional allocation is quite different from the production categories; and its inclusion produces an over-all energy investment pattern less skewed towards the producing states, as a comparison between the percentages in Tables 7 and 8, as well as between 7 and 9 suggests. The difference flows, of course, from the proportioning of energy conservation investment by households and value added in manufacturing. The mitigation of skewness is further strengthened by the fact that energy-conservation investment starts, as it were, from near zero.

Energy and Full Employment 101

It is, virtually, a new category since 1974.
The outlays for energy conservation will, therefore, be substantially incremental.

Second, evidently the major energy-producing
regions will experience (relative to population or
households) much higher levels of energy-related
investment than the others; notably, Alaska, the
Mountain states, and the West South Central region.

Putting broad generalizations aside, what can
be said more directly about the relation of an effective national energy plan to the fate of the
regions?

The Northeast and East North Central States.
This region, taken as a whole, includes half the
U. S. population. In 1960 it contained 61% of the
nation's manufacturing jobs; in 1975, 52%. This
decline, which was absolute as well as relative in
the first half of the 1970's, was accompanied, as
we all know, by acute fiscal problems in many
cities, pressures to reduce public services, a rise
in the proportion of obsolescent plant, and a de-
teriorating transport system. The region is also
experiencing severe chronic unemployment among
minorities in the central cities. As Table 6
indicates, the average growth rate in real earnings
for each of its sub-regions was below the national
average in the period 1971-1976. Only Maine and
New Hampshire, enjoying the flight from the metropolitan areas, experienced growth rates higher than
the national average.

The question is, therefore, to what extent
could an effective national energy policy help
arrest the process of deterioration and revitalize
the industrial north, taken as a whole?

The Northeast Governors have already decided
that energy-related investment could play a major
role to that end; and they have thrown their weight
behind an Energy Corporation for the Northeast.
Hearings shortly will be held on the project (and
other regional development banks) in the Senate.
A special study done for the project estimates
energy-related investment required in the region
for the period 1977-1985 in the range of $100-120
billion. This figure is somewhat higher than that

Table 9. Energy Conservation Investment by Regions, 1977-1985

(billions of 1976 dollars)

Census Region	Residential Conservation	Industrial & Commercial Conservation	Total Expenditures for Conservation	Percentage by Region
New England	2.65	9.81	12.46	6.2%
Middle Atlantic	8.58	30.78	39.36	19.6
South Atlantic	6.84	19.45	26.29	13.0
East North Central	8.98	43.86	52.84	26.2
East South Central	2.81	9.32	12.13	6.0
West North Central	3.74	10.36	14.10	7.0
West South Central	4.31	10.81	15.12	7.5
Mountain	1.83	3.20	5.03	2.5
Pacific	6.07	17.29	23.36	11.6
Alaska & Hawaii	0.20	0.25	0.45	0.2
Total U. S.	46.01	155.13	201.54	99.8%*

* Due to rounding, total not equal to 100.

Source: Allen Davidson and Martin L. Baughman, *op. cit.*

Table 10. Total 1977-1985 Regional Energy Investment; Per Household; and
Per Dollar Value-Added in Manufacturing*

Census Region	Total Energy-Related Investment		Total Expenditure Per Household	Expenditure Per Dollar-Value Added
	(billions of 1976 dollars)	Percentage by Regions		
New England	$ 19.28	2.8%	$ 5,286	$0.86
Middle Atlantic	71.22	10.2	6,017	1.01
South Atlantic	74.26	10.6	7,869	1.67
East North Central	97.60	14.0	7,603	0.98
East South Central	56.51	8.1	14,614	2.66
West North Central	51.74	7.4	10,042	2.20
West South Central	171.03	24.5	28,741	6.95
Mountain	81.63	11.7	32,420	10.96
Pacific	67.33	9.6	9,887	1.70
Alaska & Hawaii	8.64	1.2	30,638	14.85
Total U. S.	$699.24	98.9**	$11,022	$2.09

*   Household and value-added figures used are for the year 1974.
**   Due to rounding, total not equal to 100.

Source: Allen Davidson and Martin L. Baughman, *op. cit.* The total figure for energy related investment is an estimate of outlays required to fulfill NEP targets.

104 W. W. Rostow

in Table 10 ($90.5 billion); but, if related infrastructure is included, the total could easily reach $120 billion. The major fields identified for investment by the corporation are these: coal conversion; cogeneration and district heating; infrastructure to increase long-term coal supply; residential retrofit program; solid waste recovery; solar and alternative energy resources. Through public-private collaboration in areas where private profit incentives may not be sufficient, it is hoped that the corporation might invest over the period something of the order of $8 billion, which, with the incentive thus provided, might increase total investment by over $20 billion, providing about twice that figure in increased income and perhaps an extra 40,000 jobs per annum.

Behind the thrust of this initiative are two judgments. First, that while the battle for additional federal revenues will be fought, an extra margin of such funds is not likely to induce a regenerative process in the Northeast. Only a large self-reinforcing and sustained increase in investment will do the job; and, in present circumstances, this requires new forms of public-private collaboration in the region. Second, the problem of severe unemployment in the central cities can only be significantly ameliorated in a setting where the region as a whole regathers momentum and the demand for labor is high and rising. Without that condition, additional funds channelled directly to the central cities will be pushing on a string. No one believes that the hard core problem of central city unemployment can be totally and promptly eliminated by a sharp expansion of regional investment; but there is ample evidence that it could be substantially reduced; and, in such a framework, where the hard core problem was reduced and isolated, more narrowly targetted programs might have a chance to yield benign results over a longer time span.

The larger objectives of the energy effort envisaged in the Northeast, aside from additional employment, are to reduce dependence on imported oil; to assure a reliable regional energy supply and thereby remove one of the inducements for movement of facilities to energy production regions; to reduce, by conservation, the income (or terms of trade) burden of high energy prices; and to acquire, by increased energy production, some of the income (or terms of trade) advantages of such production in an era of high-priced energy.

It should be noted that the Northeast Governors were the first public officials to recognize the connection between a vigorous attack on the energy problem and the problem of chronic unemployment and slow growth.

With one addition, a similar rationale would apply in the industrial Middle West where the Governors have also thrown their support behind a regional development bank. The additional dimension in the region flows from the fact that it contains vast deposits of Devonian shale. If these resources can be brought into commercial production, perhaps with some initial public subsidy, the economic prospects for the industrial North as a whole and the nation would be altered substantially for the better.

As an economic historian I would note that rapid increases in productivity and reductions in cost of production have generally followed the introduction into commercial production of new methods and the exploitation of new raw material sources.

The Northeast and industrial Middle West have a further stake in the acceleration of what are conventionally referred to as post-1985 technologies. Aside from nuclear power, coal is the major regional energy source. Its enlarged use is likely to increase the substantial air pollution problems of the region despite environmental regulations. In situ conversion of coal and shale as well as the conversion of coal into synthetics would, it is to be hoped, mitigate this problem.

If national policy faces up to the acceptance of marginal cost energy pricing and establishes machinery for the prompt settlement, on national terms, of energy-environment trade-offs, I am inclined to believe regional development banks can perform a powerful catalytic role. That role would be in accelerating the solution to R&D problems and in overcoming uncertainties which inhibit commercial production from so-called post-1985 energy technologies; e.g., deep lignite, shale, synthetics, geopressurized methane, and geothermal.

The Mountain States. The rise in energy prices is producing in the Mountain states all four of the phenomena which emerged from the historical cases briefly summarized in Part II of this paper: an income (or terms of trade) effect; enlarged investment; accelerated in-migration; and the beginning of a new phase of energy-related industrialization. It is not surprising that Denver is being referred to as the new Houston.

A good deal of the momentum in the region flows, of course, from the beginnings of the exploitation of the massive coal deposits of the northern mountain states. A preliminary analysis indicates that "moderately firm plans" in four centers of coal development in Montana, North Dakota, and Wyoming will lead to an expansion of population at those sites between 1970 and 1985 by some 64,000 people (185%).[30] This includes some calculation of working force required for supporting private and public services, including transport. Over-all, the annual average rate of population growth of these three states was 1.34% between 1970 and 1975, 3.1% for the Mountain states as a whole. If that rate were to persist for another decade, their population would rise from 9.6 to 13.0 million.

The relative rise in incomes, investment levels, and population in the region, already evident in Tables 6 and 7, are likely to be accompanied, over a period of time, by a new phase of industrialization based on the reliability and accessibility, with low transport costs, of energy supply.

Like other regions that have struck it rich in the past, the boom in the Mountain states will transform the way of life of a good many now thinly populated parts of the region, impose considerable

---

30. Richard Nehring, Benjamin Zycher, with contributions from Joseph Wharton, *Coal Development and Government Regulation in the Northern Great Plains: A Preliminary Report,* Santa Monica: The Rand Corporation, August 1976, p. 122.

Energy and Full Employment   107

environmental costs, and set up strains between the old and new lines of economic activity. State severance and other taxes are designed to tap off some current income from the exploitation of natural resources to support both public infrastructure requirements and to cushion the environmental impact of accelerated development.

The scale of the available coal reserves of the region provides a base for a long-term process of development, in which a working force mobilized initially to build infrastructure, synthetic plants, etc. is likely to have the opportunity to move over into industrial employment and the services required to support it.

West South Central. This region, containing a good deal of the conventional oil and gas reserves of the country, faces a somewhat more complex future than the Mountain region. In one way or another it is likely to experience, for a time, a rise in domestic energy prices, enlarged investment flows, and continued rapid in-migration. The prospect is heightened by the delay since 1974 in establishing a viable national energy plan. That delay makes it probable that the nation will require a very rapid expansion of conventional onshore and Gulf reserves, since these have relatively short periods of gestation (see Chart 2, p. 20 above). These reserves are, however, believed to be limited -- more limited than, say, the coal reserves of the Mountain states. The industrial structure of the oil and gas producing states is built substantially around energy-intensive industries historically dependent on a reliable regional energy supply.[31] Forty percent of the natural gas consumed in the United States for industrial purposes, for example, is consumed in Arkansas, Louisiana, Mississippi, and Texas. Evidently, these energy-intensive industries are important to the national, rather than merely the regional, market.

---

31. See, notably, James W. McKie, "The Effects of the Proposals for Natural Gas Pricing in the National Energy Plan on the Energy Economy of Texas," in *Preliminary Assessment of the President's National Energy Plan*, Council on Energy Resources, University of Texas at Austin, May 11, 1977, pp. 179-201.

One central task in the region is, therefore, to build an alternative energy base for the longer future. That process is already under way as a result of Texas' precocious conversion of utilities from natural gas to coal. A free intrastate market price for natural gas plus a state regulation (Docket 600) set in motion a rapid expansion of local lignite production starting in 1972. By 1985 the utilities industry in Texas may be using some 98 million tons of coal, of which 40 million will be imported from the Mountain states. Gas-generated electricity will have been reduced from 90 percent to 25 percent or less of the total.[32] This process will impose some deterioration in air quality. With the passage of time, however, the oil and gas producing states of the Southwest will not only have to exploit their surface lignite but also try to render cost-effective the development of their deeper lignite deposits, geothermal gas, the abundant supply of solar energy, and the acquisition of oil by tertiary recovery methods. The rapid rate of growth of population and income in the region may also require extensive resort to nuclear energy and the full exploitation of the region's uranium resources.

It will be a considerable strain on resources and policy both to play the critical short-run role in the national energy plan the region's resources dictate while also laying the basis for the region's long-run viability in an era when conventional oil and gas reserves will have been run down. Although the region commands a much more sophisticated and diversified economy than the members of OPEC, its underlying challenge -- to make the most of a period of transient high income in ways which will permit continued long-run growth -- bears a family relation to theirs.

The Southeast. The southern states (South Atlantic and East South Central regions) confront the future energy problem with an underlying advan-

---

32. William R. Kaiser and Hal B. H. Cooper, Jr., "The Impact of Coal Utilization in Texas under the National Energy Plan," in *National Energy Policy: A Continuing Assessment*, Council on Energy Resources, University of Texas at Austin, January 1978, pp. 121-181.

tage over New England and the mid-Atlantic states; that is, they are still enjoying some of the momentum of late-comers catching up with early-comers to industrialization, as Tables 1 and 6 suggest. Their coal resources and utility requirements, moreover, should induce considerable energy-related investment. Measured per household (Table 10), the South Atlantic investment requirement approximates that of the East North Central states; the figure for the East South Central states is higher due to the presence within that region of Louisiana. Because of the lesser role of industry in the two regions, the expenditure per dollar-value added in manufacturing is higher.

Recent analyses have emphasized that within the Sunbelt a distinction is emerging in the growth rates of energy-importing versus energy-exporting states; and this is, of course, to be expected, given the terms of trade effect and the order of magnitude difference between energy investment in the West South Central states and the others (except Louisiana).

Like the states of the Northeast and East North Central regions, the South contains a major structural poverty problem. The excellent report of the Task Force on Southern Rural Development has recently measured the scale and character of poverty in the South related to the rest of the country. In 1974 there were still 10.8 million poor southerners, 13.5 million outside the South. Relative to population, the southern poverty problem is, evidently, much greater than in the rest of the country. But the southern poor are less visible: 54% are rural; only 38% are rural outside the South.

Like the central city problems of the North (and parts of the South), more than a high level of aggregate growth is required to reduce radically hard-core rural poverty. But a background of high growth rates in the region is a necessary condition.

Although it should be emphasized again that considerable differences exist among the states of the region -- and, even, within states -- the South Atlantic and East South Central regions should be

110   W. W. Rostow

able to continue in the time ahead to narrow the gap between their levels of real income per capita and the national average, if a serious national energy program is mounted and high average growth rates maintained.

The Pacific. In terms of per capita income, the Pacific region, even putting Alaska aside, remains relatively one of the richest in the country (Table 1); and it continued to do better in growth between 1971 and 1976 than the national average of 2.4% (Table 6). Energy-related investment down to 1985, putting aside Alaska, falls in an intermediate range, a bit below the national average (Table 10). Aside from Hawaii, California, much the most populous state of the region, did least well in the period 1971-1976, with a growth rate in real earnings of 2.87% versus the regional average of 3.14%. With hydroelectric resources and the energy flow from Alaska and, perhaps, Mexico, the region's energy supply is reasonably well assured. The pace and fruitfulness of offshore drilling in the Pacific will, evidently, affect the region's income, investment, and growth pattern to a degree. It may be that other resource problems (e.g., water supply, air pollution, agricultural productivity) may prove more acute in the Pacific region over the next decade.

VI

Conclusions

Seven large conclusions flow from this analysis.

1. The effects of a shift in the relative price of energy must be analyzed, internationally and by regions, in terms of four routes of impact: on income (or terms of trade); investment; migration; industrial structure, including in the latter the effect on the momentum of leading growth sectors of the price elasticity of demand for energy. Current energy-economy models are designed in ways which preclude their gripping this process as a whole. They have also focused primarily on the long term U. S. energy problem; that is, the path to the year 2000 or thereabouts.

2. The most acute phase of the energy

problem, however, is upon us now and over the next 5-10 years when the United States and other energy importers must strive with great intensity to accommodate themselves to the probable OPEC production ceiling of the 1980's by reducing oil imports. The urgency of the problem is heightened by the long lead times at work in various key types of energy production and conservation.

3. There is a solid convergence between such an intensive effort and the task of returning the U. S. and other OECD economies to relatively full employment and high, sustained growth rates. The required expansion in energy-related investment is of an order of magnitude in the United States to make this sector a leading growth sector in the economy supplanting the consumer-oriented leading growth sectors, now decelerated, which drove forward the great OECD boom of the 1950's and 1960's and filling the investment gap which, in the United States and elsewhere, is the basis for decelerated OECD growth rates. The current investment gap (third quarter 1977) is of the order of 1.7% of GNP: the expansion of energy-related investment required between 1977 and 1985 to reduce imports to, say, 6 mboed is, at the minimum, of this order of magnitude and probably a good deal higher.

4. If we deal vigorously with the energy problem and face up also to other resource problems with degenerative characteristics (e.g., water supply, pollution control, transport, soil rehabilitation), the nation's central economic problem will cease to be unsatisfactory levels of unemployment and rates of growth, but one of investment priorities.

5. Contrary to the impression imparted by some rhetoric, energy-conservation (except nonuse) is capital-intensive. Energy-conservation investment falls, in various calculations, in the range of 22-32% of total energy-related investment required over the period 1977-1985 to reduce imports to about 6 mboed by 1985.

6. Regional growth rates, rates of population expansion, and the structural problems the regions confront are extremely diverse. The impact upon them of an effective national energy plan

will also be diverse, although the large role of energy-conservation investment mitigates the skewness which would exist if the nation's task were merely to expand energy production. Among the regions, the most acute problems lie in the Northeast and industrial Middle West. Their difficulties have not been caused by the energy crisis but thus far have been exacerbated by it. An effective national energy plan, vigorously pursued in those regions through public-private sector collaboration, could substantially mitigate their energy and deeper structural problems. Each of the other regions, including those producing and exporting energy, also faces difficult structural challenges.

7. The analysis as a whole would suggest:

a. Energy-economy model builders should move away from long run, full employment, equilibrium models towards models which would capture the anatomy of the transition confronted over the years immediately ahead including: the time dimension imposed by the probable OPEC production ceiling and by energy production and conservation lead times; the role of energy-related investment in moving the national economy back to full employment and sustained growth; the regional dimensions of the energy-economy problem.

b. Macro-model builders and prognosticators, including the Council of Economic Advisers, should introduce systematically the role of energy-related investment into their calculations; disaggregate their analyses by regions; and relate regularly the role of now degenerating resource sectors to their macro-calculations.

4

Lessons of History
and Other Countries

Joel Darmstadter

You are probing the future economic growth of the country under conditions involving full utilization of its resources--human and material. You narrow your focus to energy and contemplate the range of future expansion paths for fuel and power that might accompany growth of the overall economy. You decide, based on your awareness of past trends, that at the very least, the growth rate for consumption of energy resources will match the prospective rate of growth for the nationwide economy. Your speculations, which took place in the mid 1920s, turned out--forty years later and in a full employment environment--to have been clearly misguided. The gross domestic product increased at an average annual rate of 3.1 percent; energy consumption, at only 80 percent as fast a rate of 2.5 percent per year. This relationship signified a yearly decline in the level of the energy/GDP ratio of 0.6 percent. (See Chart I.) Had the economy and energy use grown commensurately, the country would, toward the end of the 1960s, have been consuming 17 quadrillion Btu's (Quads)--or 8-1/2 million barrels/day oil equivalent--more than it was. Did this signify energy conservation? Surely "yes"--to the extent that more productive use of energy resources contributed to this development.

This momentary--and obviously much compressed-- excursion into economic history is instructive. It serves as a useful reminder that the so-called "decoupling" of energy and economic activity that is often depicted as the future imperative for a society hitherto untouched by regard for conservation conveys, in fact, a false impression. There has hardly ever been a lockstep relationship between energy and GDP--either when energy was rising relatively faster, as it was toward the end of the nineteenth and

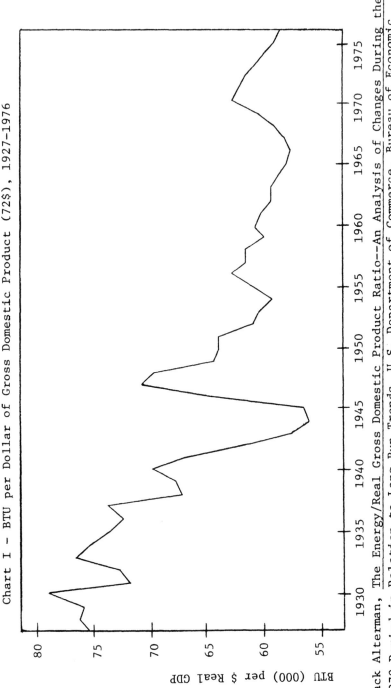

Chart I - BTU per Dollar of Gross Domestic Product (72$), 1927-1976

Jack Alterman, The Energy/Real Gross Domestic Product Ratio--An Analysis of Changes During the 1966-1970 Period in Relation to Long-Run Trends, U.S. Department of Commerce, Bureau of Economic Analysis Staff Paper No. 30, October 1977. (Updated and slightly revised.)

first two decades of the twentieth century; or when its
growth was disproportionately less, as characterizes the
overall trend during much of the ensuing period.

Past experience should give pause to those who, failing
to recognize this clearcut evidence of at least some
flexibility in the relationship of energy consumption growth
to aggregate economic growth, see no possibility of energy
trailing national output in the years ahead. One expression
of the view that energy consumption and output are activities
almost rigidly linked emerges from a recent publication of
the Chase Manhattan Bank. Ignoring the progressive long-
term decline in the U.S. energy/output ratio after the mid-
1920s, which I have referred to, the Bank asserts that the
roughly parallel trend of more recent years augurs an
enduring constancy in this relationship. It is stated that
"There is no sound, proven basis for believing a billion
dollars of GNP can be generated with less energy in the
future."[1]

The behavior of the energy/GDP ratio since the 1920s is
particularly illuminating from a conservation perspective.
For the downward trend in the ratio occurred in spite of
the steady decline in real energy prices which, all other
things equal, would have prompted an intensification of
energy use rather than the reverse. But clearly, all other
things weren't equal. This was a period during which a
number of forces acted, in their net effect, to dampen the
U.S. aggregate energy growth rate. First, the country's
heavy industrialization phase was beginning to subside--
a process implying some moderation in energy use. Second,
the years and decades following World War I witnessed a
rapid rise of electrification and this greatly enhanced the
efficiency of factory operations and the productivity of the
American worker--in spite of the fact that the generation
of a unit of electricity required a substantial multiple
thereof in primary energy inputs. But this disadvantage
was itself cushioned in a very important respect by steady
improvements in electric generating efficiency. Finally,
a significant improvement in energy conversion stemmed from
the replacement of steam locomotives by more efficient
diesel engines.

As I have indicated, these developments occurred even
while real energy prices were falling. There is another
historical sidelight which, incidentally, it is interesting

---

[1]John G. Winger and Carolyn A. Nielsen, "Energy, The
Economy, and Jobs," Energy Report from Chase (September
1976), pp. 2-3,

116   *Joel Darmstadter*

to recall. Energy prices in the late fifties and sixties could have been even lower--and consumption higher--had oil-import quotas not prevailed to restrict (then) cheap foreign oil. Indeed, the objective of lower energy prices-- and, implicitly, the enjoyment of more use--was a significant plank in the liberal politics of the time.

But to return to what actually happened, even most of the 1960-70 decade was still marked by stability in real energy prices. That situation began to change toward the end of the decade for some energy forms, and, of course, changed drastically following the sharp rise in OPEC oil prices in 1973/74. Real gasoline prices rose 22 percent and heating oil by 44 percent between those two years. Residential natural gas prices rose sharply after 1974, while electricity prices have risen moderately throughout the period. Thus, the last decade has seen a dramatic turnabout from earlier, long-term price experience. Note, however, that following the big increases in 1974, real gasoline prices have actually dropped slightly and heating oil prices have risen just a bit. One can conjecture about what additional stimulus toward conservation--and I believe there has been a clearcut recent trend towards more sparing energy use--might have ensued from sustained price pressures. One can also visualize an added conservation response if prevailing energy prices were to begin moving upward to reflect the true replacement cost of what is consumed.

II

This is a good juncture at which to try and put some precision on the term "conservation."[1] In an economic, as distinct from thermodynamic, concept, conservation signifies --well--the most economic use of energy, along with other resources, in a given process or activity, whether in the production of goods and services or in their use by ultimate consumers. An aluminum manufacturer may be able, on balance, to lower costs by introducing a process that lowers the energy requirement of an ingot produced. A homeowner may succeed in reducing heat losses through beefed-up insulation whose amortized cost is less than savings on the utility bill. Both instances satisfy the definition of conservation. It is important to emphasize that, to achieve conservation, it is not sufficient to point to reduced energy use per unit of output or activity. It is necessary to show

---

[1] Conceptual issues in energy conservation are dealt with in Lee Schipper and Joel Darmstadter, "The Logic of Energy Conservation," *Technology Review*, January, 1978.

Lessons of History and Other Countries   117

how such a change conforms to overall cost-effectiveness--
a calculation depending on the joint use of all input factors
(energy and nonenergy) and their cost in a given task.

On a nationwide level, energy consumed per unit of GDP
can, of course, decline both because important components
of GDP require less energy per unit or because the nation
shifts away from energy intensive activities--less heavy
manufacturing, more of certain kinds of personal services.
Such shifts, however, can obviously occur for reasons
unrelated to conservation impulses. Cultural activities,
for example, are desired independently of the fact that
their low energy content makes them a "good buy."
Other shifts may more directly be attributable to the
effect of higher real energy costs.

If one accepts the notion that conservation represents
monetary savings which would be foregone by doing nothing,
then certain points pertinent to the economic consequences
follow. Far from constituting a threat to output and
employment, conservation of energy--as, indeed, rational
use of all resources--is entirely in harmony with society's
concern with these measures of economic performance. Perhaps
anxiety over the nature and effects of conservation arises
from the fact that short-term disruptions requiring
emergency allocation of scarce supplies--as during the
1973/74 embargo period or the natural gas pinch in the
severe winter of 1976/77--can obviously jeopardize the
economy. But that is not because of actions or policies
chargeable to conservation. Some proponents of conservation
may also invite skepticism because of their insensitivity
to supply expansion policies which are, in my judgment, a
clearly needed complement to conservation imperatives.
The recent NAACP report on energy, for example, reflects
this skepticism.[1] But that, also, does not incriminate
the integrity of the conservation idea. Rather, it questions
policies that are perceived--rightly or wrongly--as pointing
to conservation as a least onerous, second-best solution.
One can, after all, understand subdued enthusiasm for
conservation on the part of those who see it more as a
convulsive response to managed scarcity than as an act of
economic common sense.

Relatedly, there may be apprehension--so far, I believe,
unfounded--that overly zealous public officials may at some
point be tempted to prescribe widespread maximum energy-use

---

[1]Report on NAACP National Energy Conference, Washington,
D. C., 21 December 1977. (Reprinted in *Oil Daily*, 23
January 1978.)

118 Joel Darmstadter

guidelines, I could not say that such a course would never be justified. But as a casual policy, its use might well be economically damaging. Finally, one might ask whether the administration's tendency—in unveiling the 1977 National Energy Plan—to view conservation as portending a belt-tightening, austerity regime rather than as representing beneficial opportunities to be exploited did not heighten public suspicion and confusion and generally muddy up the conservation issue. Offering tax credits as a reward for actions that are inherently profitable could compound the confusion. (By which I don't question the need for a governmental role in pursuing conservation. It's the logic of particular approaches that is debatable.)

Only in a relatively trivial, and—I believe—manageable, short-term sense does conservation connote potential injury. Fiberglass manufacturers may encroach on utility sales. (Some utilities are, perhaps not surprisingly, entering the insulation business as a subsidiary activity.) Producers of relatively energy-saving equipment may heighten their market share of the product in question. And consumer expenditure shifts may favor items in the market basket embodying less energy. And one cannot discount some regional effects: a new assembly line geared to fuel-efficient cars may displace an old one elsewhere producing traditional models. But it is hard to envision deep disruption stemming from such impacts. Indeed, even in the short-term, the net disruption may be less than these initial effects as some resources succeed in migrating to fields that are expanding or subject to capacity limitations—e.g., production of insulating material. Still, some adjustment problems will materialize.

III
Conservation, in short, insures a level of welfare above that implied in its absence. But it is certain that, even with conservation, welfare is nonetheless less than it was before an event, such as a drastic energy price increase, that prompted a change in an energy-using activity. A warehousing operation conducted under economically optimal conditions may face new choices in the balance of advantage between, say, the use of forklift trucks and conveyers, on the one hand, and the use of laborers, on the other, once increased energy prices shift the cost relationship between these two inputs. The enterprise may conceivably conclude that the new circumstances argue for employing more labor, less energy. But the economic attractiveness of the operation, while maximized at the new conditions, may be below its pre-existing level.

Lessons of History and Other Countries   119

Also, we need to keep in mind implications that may emerge in going from an individual "micro" unit of observation to an economy-wide level of abstraction. Picture a fully employed economy in which producers outbid each other in substituting labor (or some other resource) for energy. The process of adjusting to higher energy costs <u>will</u> occur at the expense of at least some decline in the <u>level</u> of output. The relevant consideration is whether more economic output or welfare is sacrificed by attempting difficult substitutions of nonenergy for energy resources or by attempting to absorb higher real energy costs.[1]

Obviously, therefore, conservation does not justify indifference to higher real energy costs since it principally cushions the severity of their impact. Nor, however, does some inescapable economic burden stemming from higher real costs warrant opposition to allowing energy prices to move up to replacement cost levels. The apparent contradiction is resolved with the recognition that price controls below market levels are themselves responsible for a sacrifice in welfare and distortions in the economy. Refiners unable to get controlled domestic oil must buy OPEC oil at world prices. New customers unable to get gas hook ups opt for much more costly electric heating. Efficient resource allocation, in general, is compromised.

IV

One issue related to this discussion has to do with the impact of changing lifestyles upon energy consumption-- a matter of wide interest. I raise it in the context of the economic effects of conservation because of the demonstrable proposition that there <u>are</u> adaptations-- mostly behavioral--that save energy with virtually no negative effects. This has "good news/bad news" aspects. The "good news" part arises from the fact that a significant portion--nearly 30 percent--of U.S. energy demand occurs in the form of direct consumption for personal use. In this segment of energy consumption, one cannot really argue that any deceleration in the growth of energy use beyond that governed by cost-effective criteria necessarily jeopardizes welfare and the economy. To be sure there are gradations in the ease with which people comfortably change their way of doing things (and it is these blurred lines of demarcation that give rise to the problem I will come to in a moment). Turning off lights in unoccupied rooms is no doubt regarded as less burdensome than avoiding the car for all trips of less than a mile. Still, it is important to

---

[1]On the question of substitutability, see Alan Manne's contribution to this volume.

Table I

PER CAPITA ENERGY CONSUMPTION AND PER CAPITA GROSS
DOMESTIC PRODUCT, NINE DEVELOPED COUNTRIES, 1972

| Country | Per capita | | Energy/GDP ratio (thousand Btu/$) | Index numbers (U.S.=100) | | Energy/GDP ratio |
| | GDP (dollars) | Energy (million Btu) | | Per capita | | |
				GDP	Energy	
United States	5,643	335.5	59.5	100	100	100
Canada	4,728	336.6	71.1	84	100	120
France	4,168	133.1	31.9	74	40	54
Germany	3,991	165.6	41.5	71	49	70
Italy	2,612	95.7	36.6	46	29	62
Netherlands	3,678	188.1	51.1	65	56	86
United Kingdom	3,401	152.9	45.0	60	46	76
Sweden	5,000	213.4	42.7	89	64	72
Japan	3,423	116.6	18.1	61	35	57

Note: The hydro and nuclear component of primary energy consumption is converted into Btu's on the basis of fuel inputs into fossil-fueled power plants, assuming 35 percent efficiency. Foreign GDPs are expressed in dollars, using a real purchasing-power basis of comparison rather than market exchange rates.

Source: J. Darmstadter, J. Dunkerley, and J. Alterman, How Industrial Societies Use Energy: A Comparative Analysis (Baltimore: © The Johns Hopkins University Press for Resources for the Future, 1977).

recognize that energy use in this sector represents the "proceeds" of income growth (which persons deploy on such things as passenger transportation and household fuels and power) rather than the "springboard" for growth through its role in the productive process. Thus, it is mostly in the other 65 percent of yearly energy use going to the business sector--industry, freight transportation, agriculture, and commercial enterprises--where energy constraints are potentially much more damaging. (The balance of 5 percent goes to government.)

The "bad news" side of the picture is that the personal segment of national energy use makes a very tempting target for the assertion of value judgments--that is, for prescribing "innocuous" behavioral and lifestyle changes that save energy. Cost-effective adaptation to the new energy price realities--through better insulation, use of heat pumps, more efficient appliances, attention to solar possibilities--is one thing. Energy menus that guarantee human satisfaction are quite another. These seem to me to be about as useful--or mischievous--as demonstrating that, nutritionally, the individual can thrive very nicely, thank you, on a diet of cottage cheese and kidney beans. Self indulgence in energy use, no less than in other pursuits, ought not to be denied the individual willing to incur the cost. Automatic transmissions in automobiles are about as "necessary" or "unnecessary" as beef or chicken, or as strawberry cheesecake.

V

Finally, some comments on the relevance, to the United States, of energy consumption patterns in foreign countries. It is an undeniable fact that, relative to levels of per capita income or GDP, per capita energy consumption in a number of other advanced industrial societies--e.g., Germany, Sweden, France--falls considerably below that in the United States. (See Table I.) This phenomenon has prompted some persons to suggest that the United States could shift to drastically reduced levels of energy use without impinging on economic activity. In a recently completed study at Resources for the Future, we found that intercountry variability in energy/GDP ratios is a very much more complex affair than is implied in such assertions.[1]

At the very least, diagnosis must precede prescription. And what the diagnosis discloses is that any effort to probe into the reasons for differences in energy/GDP ratios must

---

[1]Darmstadter, et. al., How Industrial Societies Use Energy, op. cit.

122   Joel Darmstadter

make a clearcut differentiation between (1) the compositional and structural differences among countries; and (2) the energy-intensity differences that characterize given energy using processes in the various countries. It turns out that about 40 percent of the difference between the (high) U.S. energy/GDP ratios and the (lower) foreign ratios is due to the first of these factors--the compositional and structural features. This refers to such U.S. characteristics as the large size of the country and dispersed population patterns, both of which give rise to the long distances over which goods and people move; or the preference for large, single family homes. These are clearly deeply rooted features of American society that are not easily changed--certainly not in less time than the decades it would take to substantially replace the housing stock and settlement patterns.

Parenthetically, the point about structure can be illustrated by noting that Canada, even allowing for the cold climate, uses more energy relative to income than we do. This come about largely because of the country's specialization in such energy-intensive activities as metallurgy, pulp and paper manufacturing, and chemicals production. Yet who would suggest that Canada, whose orientation to such activities derives from historically cheap hydropower and abundant natural resources, would do well to ponder the more energy-sparing character of her southern neighbor?

About 60 percent of the energy/GDP difference between the U.S. and the typical West European country situation arises from energy-intensity differences--the fact, for example, that the fuel economy of American cars has histor- ically been very much poorer and that energy consumption per unit of output in a wide range of manufacturing enterprises is distinctly higher. These contrasting energy intensities immediately force us to recognize that foreign energy prices--particularly for motor fuel but for other products as well--have traditionally been much higher. In part, these cost differences arise because, through taxation of energy (as well as of energy-using equipment), European prices are held above the market level; while in the U.S., through controls, they are held below. In both cases, social policy has intruded to help shape energy patterns--deterring use in the first case, encouraging it in the second case.

When one takes account of these cost differences, high U.S. energy intensities need not, and frequently do not, imply economically inefficient or wasteful practices. A

Lessons of History and Other Countries 123

foreign manufacturing concern that produces a unit of polyvinylchloride with 20 percent less energy, given energy costs more than 25 percent higher than here (which has been the case), is not necessarily demonstrating greater sophistication. Certainly, more would need to be known about the comparative use of all resources in the production process. It is equally clear that a precondition for approaching lower foreign energy intensities is that we begin to accept energy prices that reflect their real value, as measured by replacement cost. It has been estimated that these real resource costs may have been a third higher than prevailing prices for electricity, one-half higher for oil, and well over 100 percent higher for natural gas toward the end of 1977.[1] Viewed from this vantage point, U.S., as compared to foreign, energy consumption has been as wasteful--or prudent--as lobster dinners were before big increases in their prices began to spur a measure of self-restraint.

One should add that, even where the data point to one country's energy use as more effective than another's, that fact need not define the best attainable practice. U.S. freight transportation is, overall, less energy intensive than Western Europe's. Yet, U.S. energy intensity in freight might be even lower if, for example, ICC regulations did not dictate an empty backhaul for a northbound trucker of Georgia pecans. Similarly, more economical Swedish heating practices could be still further enhanced if occupants of unmetered apartments served by district heating did not use windows as thermostats!

In short, then, do international comparisons point to the potential for significantly reduced energy consumption without sacrifice of economic welfare? It would certainly be presumptuous to conclude that we have nothing to learn from foreign energy using practices, especially where these represent an adaptation to the high energy costs which, at least selectively, are now beginning to confront us here as well. But we would delude ourselves, if in looking at aggregate energy/GDP ratios in other countries, we were to conclude that these provide a formula for painlessly lowered energy consumption.

VI

To sum up: one's reading both of historical trends and intercountry comparisons does suggest that there is scope for long-term flexibility in the relationship between energy

---

[1]See Schipper and Darmstadter, "The Logic of Energy Conservation," op. cit.

consumption and economic activity. An upward course for relative energy prices, gradual changes in the economic and social complexion of the country, and technological developments, can all contribute to depressing the energy growth rate below the economic growth rate--perhaps substantially so. Conservation, properly defined, has a clearcut role to play in this unfolding process, and its consequences are much more apt to be beneficial than harmful to the economic welfare of society.

5

Post-Petroleum Prosperity

Denis Hayes

Dollar for dollar, an investment of more than 200 billion dollars in increasing the energy efficiency of U.S. buildings, industries, and the transportation system would save more energy than the same expenditure on new energy facilities would produce.1/ Continued, unbridled growth in per capita fuel consumption can only imperil the developed world, and "anticipated conservation" should be a keystone of Third World development. Ironically, the fossil fuels we now devour at the rate of one million barrels every ninety minutes are composed of the leftover food of that prime example of immoderate growth -- the dinosaur. Rather than learning from history's mistakes, we are burning the evidence.

Energy conservation was not well understood or widely appreciated in the early-to-mid-seventies. John Sawhill, Head of the Federal Energy Administration, advocated a gasoline tax as an energy conservation measure and was soon drawing unemployment; the Chase Manhattan Bank produced a study purporting to show that there was no significant potential for conservation in the United States.

With the dawn of 1977, the country appeared to be undergoing a sea-change. President Carter announced that conservation would be the cornerstone of his national energy policy; oil imports were inching toward the alarming 50 percent figure; the nuclear and synthetic fuels industries had long since ceased exuding much optimism that they could ever produce low-cost energy; and the public was clearly fed up with four years of federal fumbling on energy. The time seemed ripe for change.

We have now fumbled around for another year. The new administration's much-heralded energy plan contained several praiseworthy elements, but its cornerstone was excavated

125

from the Project Indepedence quarry: doubling coal production by 1985, and boosting the nuclear industry out of
its doldrums. The heart of the conservation program was
a complicated set of taxes and rebates that failed to arouse
public enthusiasm, triggered an extraordinary wave of opposition from the energy industry, and ensured that much of
the bill would fall under the jurisdiction of the Senate
Finance Committee where it was greeted with a noteworthy
lack of enthusiam.2/

Someone persuaded the President to go on national television, selling energy efficiency on the basis of "sacrifice" instead of "benefits", on the basis of "discomfort"
instead of "more jobs", and the concept sunk in public opinion like a lead balloon. The AFL-CIO came out for sustained
energy growth; the NAACP denounced energy conservation; and
the general public -- although buying record numbers of
small cars, planting record numbers of home gardens, and
purchasing residential insulation as fast as it can be
produced -- began casting a skeptical eye toward Washington,
D.C. In summary, the momentum that seemed to be gathering
behind a strong federal conservation program has stalled.
This may, therefore, be a good time to step back a few
paces to re-examine the case for conservation.

Most countries assume that their fuel requirements will
continue to grow for the foreseeable future. If the need
for an eventual energy ceiling is admitted, the day of reckoning is always thought to lie beyond the horizons of official projections. In chart form, the expected growth in
fuel requirements is frequently depicted as an expanding
wedge, still winging exponentially skyward in the last year
of the forecast.

Such studies, and there have been scores, do not
generally cap an in-depth examination of a spectrum of alternative policies. They make no attempt to grapple with the
question, "What can be?" They ask only, "Where do we seem
to be heading?" Projections are judgments made today about
tomorrow using data gathered yesterday.3/

This process of gazing into a rear-view mirror and proclaiming it to be a crystal ball necessarily results in
certain analytical hazards. "Trend is not destiny," as Rene
Dubos has phrased the problem. Unsustainable trends -- by
their very nature -- lead to discontinuities.

During the last twenty-five years, world fuel consumption tripled, oil and gas consumption quintupled, and electricity use grew almost seven-fold. Clearly, such trends cannot be sustained indefinitely -- nature abhors exponential curves as well as vacuums.

A debate is raging over the size of the world's oil and gas resource base, but conventional wisdom is increasingly pessimistic. Resource estimates are frequently conveyed in terms of the years left until world production will "peak", with some responsible estimates suggesting we have less than a decade. If true, a Volvo bought today may still be on the road when world oil production peaks. If the government of Saudi Arabia were to decide it would prefer to have oil in the ground than paper money in the bank, the peak could theoretically come as early as next year.4/

The range of possible energy options is narrowed by factors other than just the scarcity of certain fuels. Long before all the earth's coal has been burned, for example, coal use will be halted by the impact of rising atmospheric carbon dioxide levels on climate. Solar energy will not "run out" for billions of years, but some solar technologies will be limited by a scarcity of the materials needed to build devices to capture and store the energy in sunlight.5/

In both the Third World and the industrialized world, various physical limits on energy growth have begun to assert themselves. Mountains are denuded by scavengers in a desperate quest for firewood, and ever-hungry draft animals have little surplus energy for tilling the fields. The growing demands of an expanding population push traditional energy systems past their carrying capacities -- leading in some cases to ecological collapse. In the developed nations, a lack of water in the American West, a scarcity of suitable land in The Netherlands, and a lack of healthful air over much of Japan have all acted as brakes on energy growth.6/

In addition to such physical limits, energy supplies are also influenced by social factors. Despite the best efforts of powerful supporters in all quarters, energy growth is already pressing against social limits in much of the industrial world. Farmers are opposing strip mines; environmentalists are fighting petroleum refineries; and skyrocketing construction have led to the cancellation of plans for many nuclear reactors.

Every energy source is under the heels of both physical and social constraints. Some such limits are absolute -- when natural gas runs out, natural gas consumption must stop -- but more often they manifest themselves as increasingly severe hindrances on growth. Depending upon the mix of technologies employed, different types of constraints will come into play, but at some point accumulated constraints will halt further energy growth completely.

The case for energy conservation should not be argued in purely negative terms. A comprehensive program of energy conservation initiated today will allow the earth's limited resource base of high-quality fuel to be stretched. It will enable our descendants to share in the earth's finite stock of fossil fuels. It will make an especially critical difference to those living in underdeveloped lands where the marginal benefit per unit of fuel used is far greater than it is in highly industrialized countries.

Energy conservation will allow a portion of the fossil fuel base to be reserved for non-energy purposes: drugs, lubricants, and other materials. The energy cost of manufacturing such substances from carbon and hydrogen when our existing feedstocks have been exhausted could be astronomical.

Energy conservation will allow us to minimize the environmental degradation associated with all current energy conversion technologies. It will decrease the odds that we will cross climatic thresholds, triggering consequences that may be devastating. It will provide the opportunity to avoid reliance upon objectionable energy sources while the search for safe, sustainable sources continues.

Energy conservation could lead to more exercise, better diets, less pollution, and other indirect benefits to human health. An enlightened program of energy conservation will substantially bolster employment levels. And the security of a modest energy budget is more easily assured than that of an enormous one that depends upon a far-flung network of sources.7/

But what will energy conservation mean for that preeminent touchstone of public policy: the economy? Is it true, as is apparently felt by important segments of society, that a reining-in of our energy growth -- however attractive it may be from some perspectives -- would have a wholly negative impact on the economy?

Comparisons between countries and between different facilities in the same country make it clear that reducing industrial fuel consumption need not reduce economic output. Consumption cutbacks require only the increased use

Post-Petroleum Prosperity   129

of fuel-efficient industrial machinery and the improved operation and maintenance of this machinery. Cutbacks may also lead to the substitution of capital, materials, labor, or ingenuity for energy, or to a shift in the mixture of goods and services produced.8/ For the past fifty years, the amount of fuel consumed per dollar's worth of goods and services produced has fallen -- despite declining real energy prices. With rising energy prices a near-certainty for the foreseeable future, this trend could accelerate dramatically.9/

Energy conservation has traditionally been among industry's lowest priorities. Fuel has been so inexpensive that extravagant fuel use has gone unquestioned; moreover, energy prices (adjusted for inflation) fell steadily for decades, and popular mythology held that future sources would eventually be "too cheap to meter." Industrial energy efficiency has nonetheless improved over the years, mostly through rather unimaginative advances.

Conserving industrial energy used to mean just eliminating embarrassing waste. For example, when it had infrared photographs taken of a facility to detect heat leaks, the Dow Chemical Company discovered that a sidewalk heating system used to clear pathways of snow had been left on in summer. The company "conserved" energy by flipping a switch that had been left on by accident. Other companies accomplished major savings by repairing broken windows and closing huge, two-story factory doors.

The biggest opportunities for fuel savings, however, require more sophistication. Devices such as recuperators, regenerators, heat wheels, and heat pipes, for example, help conserve the heat generated in industrial plants, heat that would otherwise be used once and discharged or removed directly with the flue gases without having been used at all.10/

Particularly impressive gains can be made in the primary metals industries. Energy savings of over 50 percent can be made in the steel industry if older plants are gradually replaced by more efficient facilities. For example, continuous casting holds a large energy advantage over ingot pouring, and major differences exist in the efficiencies of different types of blast furnaces. In addition, hot coke is at present often quenched with water -- a method that wastes energy while producing enormous amounts of air and water pollution. In plants in Europe and in the Soviet Union, coke is cooled with a recycled inert gas, and much of its heat is recaptured to perform useful work.11/

130   Denis Hayes

The manufacture of aluminum is so energy-intensive that the industry has generally situated its major installations near sources of large amounts of cheap electricity. Technical advances in the traditional Hall aluminum refining process can reduce energy requirements by more than a fifth; Alcoa is now building a major facility using a new chloride process that is expected to reduce energy needs by almost one-third.

The paper and cement industries also make inefficient use of energy. The most efficient paper-manufacturing technologies require 50 percent less fuel than other commonly used methods need. If, in addition to embracing more efficient conventional technologies, industry were to use all wood wastes as fuel, Swedish-style, some paper factories' demand for fossil fuels could be slashed by an astonishing 75 percent. In cement manufacturing in the United States, an average of 1.2 million Btus is used to decompose enough limestone to produce a barrel of cement. In some European plants, where waste heat from cement kilns is recaptured to preheat the limestone feedstock, only 550,000 Btus are needed per barrel.12/

An important part of increasing the energy efficiency of industry will be matching energy sources of different qualities to appropriate uses. The lower-grade heat that remains after high-grade energy is used should be recaptured and used to perform other work. This process of using energy at each of the thermodynamic stages of decreasing usefulness through which it passes is termed "cascading."

At present, electricity fulfills much of industry's energy demand. In the United States, electricity constitutes about one-third of all industrial energy, and most of this electricity is purchased from large centralized power plants. The average efficiency of American power plants is below 30 percent; fully 70 percent of the energy originally contained in the fuel they use is discharged into the environment as low-grade heat. But factories have many needs for low-grade heat, needs they now meet by burning high-grade fuels. If electrical generation took place inside factories instead of at remote power plants, the waste heat could be efficiently cascaded through multiple uses.

A study performed for the National Science Foundation recommended that the United States install at least 50,000 megawatts of industrial co-generation capacity by 1985. The study pointed out that such investments require far less capital and fuel per unit of electricity produced than do investments in new centralized power plants.13/

Industrial energy conservation is not always cheap to implement. The capital required for major retooling in industry can, on the contrary, sometimes be substantial. Because society does not have an endless supply of capital, major investments of one type necessarily foreclose other options. Today, about one-fourth of all new capital investment goes into energy production. Consequently, competition exists between the financial requirements of new energy facilities and the capital needed for improvements in industrial energy efficiency. For example, the original United States proposal for Project Independence would have required about $1 trillion by 1985, four-fifths of which would have been earmarked for new, rather than replacement, energy facilities. If spent on energy production, this money would necessarily not be available for other industries, transportation, housing, and so forth. Major investments must be made in all these sectors if they are to convert to more energy-efficient processes. The pool of available capital is limited, and large-scale investments in new energy facilities can be made only by using money that could more fruitfully be invested in increased efficiency. If, as Gregory Bateson contended, capital is the "stored flexibility" necessary for any structural transformation, society would greatly narrow its industrial options by investing too heavily in new energy facilities.14/

Within some limits, a commercial enterprise can be adjusted to achieve any of several different goals: it can maximize profits, employment, output, or security. The energy industries have largely sought to maximize growth, often at the expense of other objectives. To encourage growth, rates and prices have been structured in ways that reward high consumption. They have conveniently ignored most environmental and health costs.

From the viewpoint of the energy producer, investments in growth have a substantial advantage over investments in conservation: new facilities produce a tangible, salable product. Although the same amount of money invested in conserving energy would often save more energy than can be produced by investments in new facilities, this conserved energy (which would otherwise be wasted) is energy that has already been counted by the producer as sold. The energy company and its stockholders, for whom a dollar burned is a dollar earned, are generally unenthusiastic about "returned merchandise."

132   *Denis Hayes*

The understandable drive to sell increasing amounts of energy has unfortunate consequences. For example, electric utilities have no incentive to match energy types with appropriate uses. Because they sell only electricity, electricity is hawked for all uses. Utilities first encouraged extravagant consumption for appropriate uses of electricity (e.g., lighting). Later, they began pushing inappropriate uses (e.g., resistance heating) as well.

For most artificial lighting, no better energy source than electricity exists. But artificial lighting itself often becomes too much of a good thing. Lighting requirements were minimal until the industry lobbied tirelessly to shed more and more light on things. William Lam, a Massachusetts architect and lighting consultant, has described how lighting standards for U.S. schools rose from three foot-candles in 1910, to eighteen by 1930, to thirty by 1950, to between seventy and 150 today. Similar increases took place in office buildings, hospitals, and other public buildings. Supporting this view of "manufactured demand" for public lighting is the fact that lighting levels in the home, where personal choice can be exercised, are far lower than in commercial buildings or schools.15/

Lights give off more heat than illumination. The most efficient fluorescent lamps convert only about 20 percent of the electricity they use into light, casting off the remainder directly as heat. And incandescent bulbs are only about one-third as efficient as fluorescent ones. By the lates 1950s, so much heat was being generated by the lights in some commercial buildings that air conditioning was needed even in winter. Every three watts of unnecessary lighting requires the use of one additional watt for cooling. Over half the air conditioning load in many offices is needed to combat the heat generated by light.

A society intent upon reducing its fuel consumption can turn to both technical solutions and social solutions. Technical solutions require essentially no behavioral alterations -- merely changes in the types of machinery we utilize, or in the way we use it. Social solutions, on the other hand, require changes in the way people live and act.

Two basic kinds of technical approaches are leak plugging and machine switching. Leak plugging eliminates the waste in existing technologies, while machine switching involves the replacement of existing devices with more efficient ones. To insulate a house is to plug a leak; to replace an electrical resistance furnace with a heat pump is to switch machines. To tune up a car is to plug a leak; to trade it in for a more fuel-efficient model is to switch machines.

A less obvious kind of technical solution involves the careful thermodynamic matching of the task at hand with the energy sources best able to perform it without generating waste. Preliminary studies in several countries have uncovered enormous inefficiencies; useful energy is habitually treated as a waste product and discharged into the environment. A group of physicists who scrutinized the efficiency of U.S. energy use in terms of the Second Law of Thermodynamics for the American Physical Society pegged the country's overall thermodynamic efficiency at between 10 and 15 percent. Cars were found to be 10 percent efficient, home heating 6 percent, air conditioning 5 percent, and water heating only 3 percent efficient.16/

A thermodynamic efficiency of 100 percent is an idealized and impossible standard. Moreover, decisions cannot be made on the basis of thermodynamic efficiency alone; economic costs, environmental costs, and the costs of human time must all be balanced in a wise strategy. Nonetheless, an efficiency as low as 10 to 15 percent should raise eyebrows. Doubling it to a mere 20 or 30 percent would cut the U.S. energy budget in half without changing anything other than the usefulness of machines and processes, and recent studies confirm that such a move is economically practical at current prices.17/

Every country uses most of its energy as heat. In many, heat comprises over 90 percent of energy demand, while in the United States the figure ranges closer to 60 percent. In industrialized countries, much of this heat is obtained by burning fossil fuels at very high temperatures -- often to heat water or air to less than 100 degrees C. Even worse, these fuels are often converted at 40 percent efficiency or less into electricity, which, after transmission and distribution losses, is used in domestic hot-water heaters. Using electricity to heat water is akin to killing houseflies with a cannon; it can be done, but only with a lot of messy, expensive, and unnecessary side effects. It would be much more thermodynamically efficient to reserve the high-temperature heat and electricity for tasks that require them, and to use residual heat for lower-grade purposes, like heating water.

134 *Denis Hayes*

Finally, finite fuels can be replaced by sustainable
energy sources, drawing upon the natural flows of energy
that will circulate through the biosphere whether or not
they are tapped by human beings. At present, we tend to
ignore the sun and the wind as power sources, or to use
our fossil fuels to resist their effects. Instead, we
could harness them to meet human energy requirements.

Probably the strongest single impetus for technical
approaches to conservation has been economic. In both
industrialized and rural societies, a dollar invested in
energy conservation can make more net energy available than
a dollar invested in developing new energy supplies. In
the United States, for example, investments in improving
air conditioner efficiency can save ten times as much
electricity as similar investments in new power plants can
produce. Similarly, a $10 investment in improved stove
efficiency can cut an Indian family's wood consumption
in half -- saving $10 to $25 per year. Neither example
entails a loss of benefit or comfort. But both save far
more energy per dollar than investments in new energy
sources could produce, and the energy saved is just as
valuable as new energy produced. The economic advantage
of such conservation speaks for itself, especially in a
period of general capital shortages.18/

The most elementary of the "social" approaches to
energy conservation might be thought of as belt tightening.
This conservation tactic generally refers to minor changes
in life-styles that are mostly neutral in their effect
on people but that are occasionally inconvenient or irritat-
ing. Belt tightening involves, for example, such things a
turning off unnecessary lights, driving cars more slowly,
and using commercial or residential heating and cooling
systems more sparingly.

Social approaches also include cooperative endeavors:
car pools, public transit systems, apartment buildings,
joint ownership or rental of infrequently used items,
and so on. A four-person car pool uses only about one-
fourth as much gasoline as do four cars driving the same
distance, and most apartment house walls, since they are
shared, retard heat loss to the outdoors.

The final social approach to energy conservation involves exchanging energy-intensive devices for those
that require less energy. The evolution of living habits
is already evident in the general shift of most industrial
societies from an emphasis on goods to an emphasis on ser-

Post-Petroleum Prosperity   135

vices. It could now lead to the substitution of low-energy activities like gardening or education for high-energy activities. Their proponents frequently refer to low-energy life-styles as "living lightly on the earth." Undertaken by entire societies, such social changes could cut fuel consumption by reshuffling the components of the GNP.

Consumption patterns for commercial fuels, after two decades of unbroken exponential growth, have changed radically over the last four years. Even more fundamental discontinuities seem likely in the near future. Momentous conflicts loom between habits and prices, between convenience and vulnerability, between the broad public good and narrow private interests. The political conflicts surrounding the conservation provisions of the proposed National Energy Act provide some insight into what we might expect. An urgent national effort, aimed at substituting conservation investments for production investments wherever it makes economic sense at the margin, will not be achieved without a struggle.

The electrical utilities and the oil industry, whose business it is to whet and then fill the national energy appetite, accumulated an impressive string of legislative victories. Their lobbyists were spectacularly successful at watering down key conservation provisions and at inserting massive tax credits for nuclear and synthetic fuel investments.

The Carter Administration in contrast ignored the jurisdictional implications of the Congressional committe system during its rushed effort to design an energy bill. It failed to bargain effectively with key members of the Senate, and made little effort to consolidate an effective political constituency for its policies. Indeed, the White House failed even to woo the support of the AFL-CIO and the NAACP -- two groups whose members could expect to benefit greatly from a strong national commitment to energy conservation.

No comprehensive conservation program can be passed unless it is tailored to ensure the support of enough powerful entities to deliver a majority of Congress. In particular, the program must be designed to become a priority goal of organized labor, farmers, city officials, and at least some fraction of the business community. None of these groups exerted any significant effort on behalf of the conservation provisions of the current bill.

A transition to an efficient, sustainable energy
system is both technically possible and socially desirable.
But 150 countries of widely different physical and social
circumstances are unlikely to undergo such a transition
smoothly and painlessly. Every potential energy source
will be championed by vested interests and fought by
diehard opponents. Bureaucratic inertia, political timi-
dity, conflicting corporate designs, and the simple, understandable reluctance of people to face up to far-reaching
change will all discourage a transition from taking place
spontaneously. Even when clear goals are widely shared,
they are not easily pursued. Policies tend to provoke
opposition; unanticipated side effects almost always occur.

If the path is not easy, it is nonetheless the only
road worth taking. For twenty years, global energy policy
has been headed down a blind alley. It is not too late to
retrace our steps before we collide with inevitable bounda-
ries. But the longer we wait, the more tumultous the eventual turnaround will be.

References

1 Roger S. Sant, "Adjusting Capital Stock to Higher Energy Using Efficiencies," in this volume.

2 Energy Policy and Planning Staff, The White House, National Energy Plan (Washington, D.C.: April 1977).

3 Herman E. Daly, Steady-State Economics (San Francisco: W. H. Freeman and Co., 1977); U.S. House of Representatives, Committee on Interior and Insular Affairs, Energy "Demand" Studies: An Analysis and Appraisal, Committee Print, September 1972.

4 Typical of the new wave of informed pessimism is the Report of the Workshop on Alternative Energy Strategies: Energy: Global Prospects 1985-2000 (New York: McGraw-Hill, 1977). The best single guide to the complex world of petroleum estimates is probably D.C. Ion, Availability of World Energy Sources (London: Graham & Trotman, Ltd., 1976).

5 Lester B. Lave and Eugene P. Seskin, Air Pollution and Human Health (Baltimore: Johns Hopkins University Press, for Resources for the Future, 1977); National Academy of Sciences, Energy and Climate (Washington, D.C.: 1977); Stephen H. Schneider with Lynne E. Mesirow, The Genesis Strategy: Climate and Global Survival (New York: Plenum Press, 1976); William W. Kellogg, "Is Mankind Warming the Earth?," Bulletin of the Atomic Scientists, February 1978; J. H. Mercer, "West Antarctic Ice Sheet and CO_2 Greenhouse Effect: A Threat to Disaster," Nature, January 26, 1978.

6 Erik Eckholm, Losing Ground: Environmental Stress and World Food Prospects (New York: W. W. Norton & Co., 1976); Denis Hayes, Rays of Hope: The Transition to a Post-Petroleum World (New York: W. W. Norton & Co., 1977).

7 Denis Hayes, Energy: The Case for Conservation (Washington, D.C.: Worldwatch Institute, 1976); Lester R. Brown, Redefining National Security (Washington, D.C.: Worldwatch Institute, 1977).

8 Joel Darmstadter, Joy Dunkerley, and Jack Alterman, How Industrial Societies Use Energy: A Comparative Analysis (Baltimore: Johns Hopkins University Press, for Resources for the Future, 1977); Thomas F. Widmer and Elias P. Gyftopoulos, "Energy Conservation and a Healthy Economy," Technology Review, June 1977; Lee Schipper and Joel Darmstadter, "The Logic of Energy Conservation," Technology Review, January 1978.

138   *Denis Hayes*

9   John C. Myers, "Energy Conservation and Economic Growth--
Are they Incompatible?," The Conference Board Record, February 1975.

10   Elias P. Gyftopoulos, Lazaros J. Lazaridis, and Thomas
F. Widmer, Potential Fuel Effectiveness in Industry, A Report
to the Energy Policy Project of the Ford Foundation (Cambridge, Mass.: Ballinger Publishing Co., 1974).

11   Hayes, Rays of Hope.

12   Ibid.

13   Dow Chemical Company, Environmental Research Institute
of Michigan, Townsend-Greenspan & Co., and Cravath, Swaine,
& Moore, Energy Industrial Center Study, draft report to the
National Science Foundation, 1975.

14   Amory Lovins, Soft Energy Paths (Cambridge, Mass.:
Ballinger Publishing Co., 1977).

15   Hayes, Rays of Hope.

16   "Efficient Use of Energy: A Physics Perspective," The
American Physical Society, January 1975 (Reprinted in ERDA
Authorization Hearings -- Part I, House Committee on Science
& Technology, February 18, 1975.

17   Marc H. Ross and Robert H. Williams, "Assessing the
Potential for Energy Conservation" (Albany, New York: The
Institute for Policy Alternatives, July 1975).

18   Hayes, Rays of Hope.

6

The Fable of the Elephant and the Rabbit?

Alan S. Manne

1. Energy-economy interactions

Much of the energy debate is centered around the issue of linkage between the energy sector and the balance of the U.S. economy. Implicitly, strong linkages are assumed both by proponents and by opponents of new energy supply technologies such as nuclear reactors and coal-based synthetic fuels. The proponents of these technologies argue that they are essential if the future rate of GNP growth is not to be slowed down. The opponents assert that the rate of growth ought to be slowed down -- precisely in order to avoid the safety and environmental consequences associated with nuclear energy and with coal.

Still another viewpoint is logically possible -- one which rejects the hypothesis of a tight linkage between energy consumption and economic growth. According to this third viewpoint, there are many ways to reduce energy consumption without having a major impact on the GNP. Typically, however, conservation is not costless. Despite much rhetoric to the contrary, conservation generally requires that we substitute other economic goods in place of energy. Three examples would be: (a) insulation to replace heating fuels in homes and other structures; (b) increased use of heat exchangers and of cogeneration within industry; and (c) the use of diesels to replace internal combustion engines in automobiles.

The author is solely responsible for the views expressed here. Much of the material, however, is based upon an earlier paper written jointly with William Hogan.

Thanks go to Dennis Fromholzer, Ray Squitieri and Sergio Granville for their assistance with these calculations.

140   Alan S. Manne

Each of these conservation measures would eventually become cost-effective if there were a sufficient rise in the price of energy. Opinions will differ on the time lags and on the magnitude of the price increase that would be needed in order to induce significant amounts of conservation. If one believes that cost-effective conservation is easy, the energy-GNP linkage is a weak one. If, however, it turns out that the converse is true, the impending exhaustion of oil and gas resources leaves the U.S. with a difficult set of choices -- either imposing heavy energy taxes and curtailing GNP growth or else actively promoting the introduction of nuclear energy and of coal-based technologies. Both solar electric and thermonuclear fusion are additional possibilities, but it seems unlikely that they can make a major contribution until 2020 or thereabouts.

2.   The elephant and the rabbit?

Much of the energy-GNP linkage debate may be summarized in terms of a difference in views on the ease of substitution (in economists' language, the "elasticity of substitution") between energy and other inputs to the economy. Unfortunately -- as we will see later -- the empirical evidence leaves room for a great deal of debate on the numerical value of this elasticity parameter.

For simplicity here, we shall represent the economy in terms of just two inputs -- energy and all other items. Note that energy is only a small component of the U.S. economy. As of 1970, the value of primary energy inputs did not exceed 4% of the GNP. At 1970 or even at current prices, this is something like an elephant-rabbit stew. If such a recipe contains just one rabbit (the energy sector) and one elephant (the rest of the economy), won't it still taste very much like elephant stew?

If prices had not risen after 1970, it is likely that energy demands would have grown at about the same rate as the GNP. The 4% ratio would then continue into the future. But what if energy costs double, and there is sufficient time for the economy to adapt to this change? A naive estimate of the impact may be obtained by assuming a constant input mix. On this basis, an additional 4% of gross output must be allocated to cover the costs of energy. Other input-mix options are in fact available, and some would lead to lower costs. Thus, the first doubling of real energy costs since 1970 would produce, at most, a 4% permanent loss in GNP.

For large price increases -- or for large reductions in the availability of energy -- it is no longer a valid approximation to suppose that the value share remains constant. To evaluate large changes, we must proceed beyond the metaphor of the elephant and the rabbit.

The elasticity of substitution concept is illustrated in Figure 1. The point identified as "current input mix" represents one possible combination of the inputs of energy and of other factors (capital and labor) used to produce a given level of total output. The lines drawn through this point indicate alternative combinations of inputs that could be used to produce the same level of output. These constant output curves summarize the potential for substitution between energy and other inputs. Three alternatives are shown in Figure 1 -- with elasticities of substitution equal to zero, one and infinity.

If the energy-GNP ratio were an immutable constant, this would imply a _zero_ elasticity of substitution. It would mean that total output could not be increased without increases in both energy and nonenergy inputs. This fixed proportions assumption flies in the face of common sense. It is reminiscent of the theories that led the U.S. and its allies to attempt to destroy the German ball bearing industry during World War II, and thereby to knock out the entire German economy.

At the opposite extreme, if all inputs to the economy were completely fungible, there would be an infinite elasticity of substitution. This also flies in the face of common sense. It would mean that machinery could run without energy, or that energy would be useful without machines.

Still another hypothesis is that the elasticity of substitution is _unity_. This would imply that with an increase in the relative price of energy, the optimal value share of energy inputs would remain constant at, say, 4% of the GNP.

Today, most econometricians would agree that σ (the elasticity of substitution) -- when measured in terms of primary energy -- is a good deal lower than unity. The implications of several alternative estimates of this parameter are illustrated in Figure 2.

For present purposes, it is reasonable to assume that primary energy demand (in terms of fossil fuel equivalents) would grow at a rate close to that of the total economy _if_ relative energy prices were to remain constant. At 3% per year growth from 1970, the GNP in 2010 would be approximately $4.4 trillions, and total primary energy inputs would be 220 quads (in terms of fossil fuel equivalents). This case is

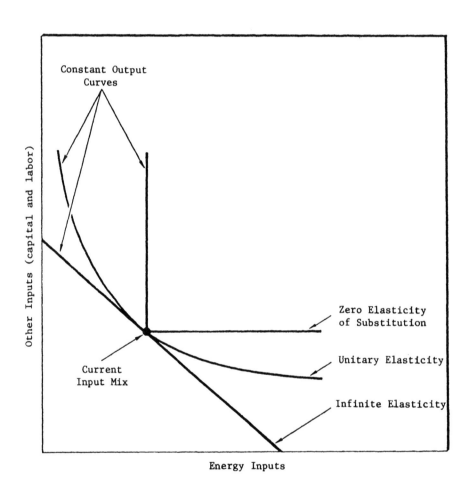

Figure 1   The Elasticity of Substitution Concept

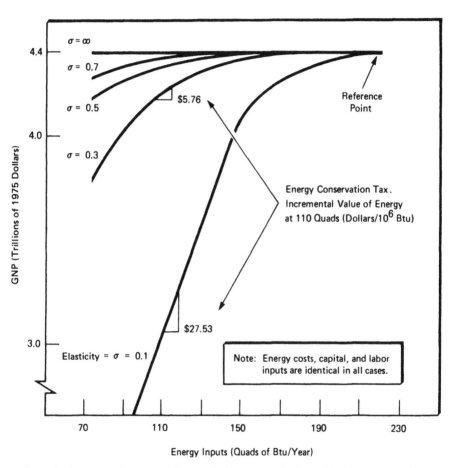

Figure 2 Economic Impacts of Energy Reductions in the Year 2010 for Various Elasticities of Substitution (σ)

Source: Hogan, W. and A. Manne, "Energy-Economy Interactions: The Fable of the Elephant and the Rabbit?" in C.J. Hitch (ed.) <u>Modeling Energy-Economy Interactions: Five Approaches,</u> Resources for the Future, Washington, D.C., 1977.

144   Alan S. Manne

shown as the "reference point" in Figure 2.

Now suppose that for reasons of resource conservation, environmental protection, or national security, there is a need to reduce energy consumption. Suppose further that the economy's inputs of capital and labor remain constant. One way to achieve the reduction in energy consumption would be through an energy conservation tax -- with the tax revenues fully redistributed in an equitable pattern. Other policy measures (e.g., auto efficiency standards) could also achieve much the same goal, but for illustrative purposes we shall simply describe all of these measures as an "energy conservation tax". This tax represents the incremental value of energy at alternative consumption levels. Under these assumptions, the feedback issue can be posed through two questions:

a) What is the size of the conservation tax?

b) What is the resulting impact on GNP?

For alternative values of σ (the elasticity of substitution), the answers to these questions are illustrated in Figure 2. This graph depicts the GNP that would result at various levels of energy input, ranging from the reference value of 220 quads down to 70 quads -- if the inputs of capital and labor are held constant, and if energy costs also remain constant. The results are shown for elasticities of substitution ranging between 0.1 and 0.7. Each of these curves is highly nonlinear. Small reductions in energy consumption may be virtually costless, but large ones are expensive.

Thus, if the elasticity of substitution is 0.3, it would require a 4.3% reduction in GNP to achieve a 50% reduction in energy consumption (110 instead of 220 quads). In percentage terms, this would be a small reduction. Nonetheless it would constitute a large absolute loss -- nearly $200 billions' worth of the GNP in that one year alone.

For policy purposes, the more relevant result may be the magnitude of the energy conservation tax. With $\sigma = 0.3$, it would require a tax of $5.76/10^6$ BTU in order to achieve this level of conservation. (The OPEC-determined price of crude oil was $2.00/10^6$ BTU in 1975.) Thus, the future tax might have to be nearly 300% of today's international energy price!

3. Empirical evidence on elasticities

Traditionally, econometric estimates of energy elasticities are based upon two sources of objective empirical data: (a) time series evidence from within a single country, and (b) intercountry or interregional "cross section" comparisons at a single point in time. There is also the possibility of pooling the evidence from these diverse sources. Each approach leads to difficulties, and there is no simple way to resolve the uncertainties.

Some of the uncertainties can be resolved by standardizing the definition of the point at which energy demands are measured. In general, elasticities are a good deal lower for "primary" energy than for "end use" demands. There are pros and cons associated with each of these points of measurement. (For further details, see Appendices C and D, Modeling Resource Group, CONAES (1977).) Throughout this paper, we employ the "primary" rather than the "end use" definition.

Figure 3 contains a typical set of time series data. It refers to the U.S. for selected years from 1947 through the first half of 1977. Energy prices are plotted against the energy-GNP ratio at different points in time. There are many pitfalls in defining what we mean by "the" price of energy and "the" energy-GNP ratio. No one statistical concept is altogether appropriate.

As the best available indicator of U.S. primary energy prices, it appears sensible to employ the domestic wellhead price of crude oil (expressed in dollars of constant 1975 purchasing power). For the other major sources of primary energy throughout this period -- coal and natural gas -- there are high transport costs and large price differences from one region of the U.S. to another. Moreover, natural gas prices have been regulated at artificially low levels during the past decade. Since the 1973 embargo, the domestic price of crude oil has also been regulated, but here the losses in economic efficiency appear less significant.

There are further difficulties in defining what we mean by the quantity of primary energy. For these rough calculations, it seems appropriate to add together oil and gas on a BTU basis. Surely this is inappropriate, however, for coal. As boiler fuels, oil and coal are virtually perfect substitutes. Nonetheless, the price that consumers have been willing to pay per BTU of coal has been consistently less than that for oil. Accordingly -- for purposes of Figure 3 -- the aggregate consumption of fossil energy has been

146   Alan S. Manne

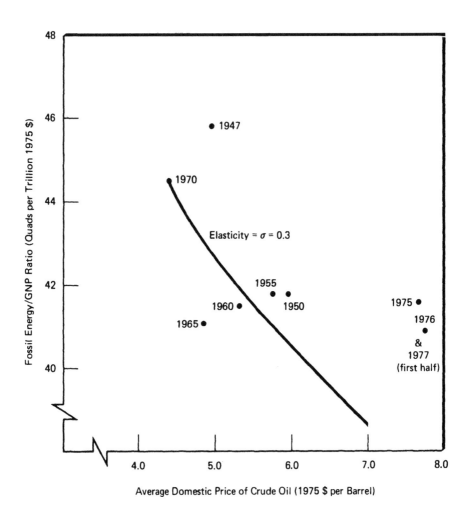

Figure 3   U.S. Time Series of Crude Oil Prices and Fossil Energy/GNP Ratios

The Elephant and the Rabbit? 147

defined as the sum of oil and gas (measured in quads), plus 70% of the quads of coal consumed in the U.S. This is sometimes termed a "value-weighted" measure of energy consumption. Further details on Figure 3 are provided in a memorandum available upon request.

Regardless of the subtleties of definition, Figure 3 shows little evidence of a close correlation between the price and the energy-GNP ratio. The ratio has varied within only a narrow band throughout this time period, and yet prices have moved over a 2:1 range. It is true that energy consumers have not yet had sufficient time to adapt their lifestyles and their stocks of durable goods to the high prices prevailing since 1973. There has, however, been only a small decrease in the energy-GNP ratio -- despite higher prices and despite greater public awareness of the need for energy conservation.

To illustrate one possible numerical estimate of elasticities, Figure 3 contains a price-quantity demand curve -- extrapolating through the 1970 (pre-embargo) point on the basis of a price elasticity of 0.3. This means that a 1% increase in energy prices would lead to a decrease of 0.3% in the energy-GNP ratio. (With this definition, the price elasticity is virtually identical in its numerical value to σ , the elasticity of substitution.) With $\sigma = 0.3$, note that the extrapolated potential for energy conservation lies well below the actual values achieved during 1975-77. This may mean that there are extremely long time lags in the process of energy conservation. Or it may mean that the long-run elasticity is lower than 0.3. If the latter conclusion holds true, there is a fairly close linkage between energy consumption and GNP growth, and it will not be easy to decouple the two.

Most of the evidence in favor of high elasticities is drawn from international cross-section analyses such as the one illustrated by Figure 4. Here Griffin (1977) has compared the energy/GNP ratio versus the per capita product in 19 OECD (high-income) countries. Note first that there is little correlation between the energy/GNP ratio and the per capita product. To a first approximation, this confirms the view that income elasticities are of the order of 1.0. That is, within a given country, a 1.0% increase of GNP will be associated with a 1.0% increase in primary energy consumption -- other things being equal.

Between countries, however, other things are not equal. Figure 4 indicates that Canada, Finland, the U.K. and the U.S. have energy-GNP ratios that are nearly twice as high as

148 Alan S. Manne

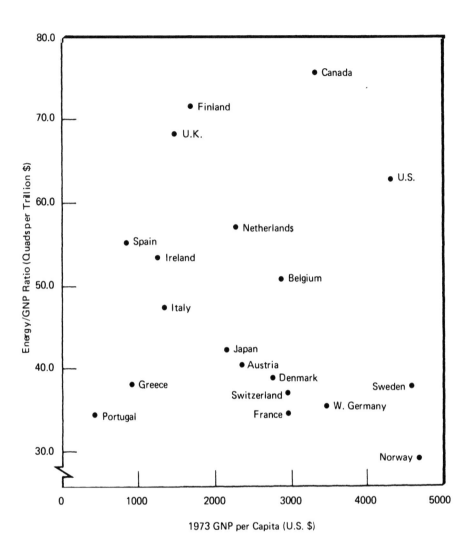

Source: Griffin (1977)

Figure 4 An International Comparison of Energy/GNP Ratios in 1973

The Elephant and the Rabbit?   149

those in Sweden and West Germany. Other countries lie between these extremes. What leads to intercountry differences
in the energy-GNP ratio? Many econometricians believe that
these are largely attributable to differences in energy tax
policies -- and hence that the intercountry variations reflect long-run adjustments to differing energy prices.

On this hypothesis, price-demand elasticities may be
inferred from intercountry comparison. E.g., Griffin's estimates are based upon a pooled time series and cross section
for the OECD countries. According to his simulations to the
year 2000, "a 2% increase in the annual increase of energy
prices reduced the (energy demand) growth rate from 4.1 to
3.2%" (p. 31, ch. VIII). This implies a price elasticity
of 0.45 -- when prices are measured at the point of end use.
In turn, this implies a considerably lower price (and substitution) elasticity of demand for primary energy.

Griffin's work suggests a somewhat lower estimate of σ
than the value of 0.40 obtained previously by Nordhaus.
(Again refer to Appendix C, Modeling Resource Group, CONAES,
1977.) Both Griffin and Nordhaus, however, omit "country
dummy" variables to explain the demand for motor gasoline.
This may well lead to an underestimate of the country-
specific factors (population densities, width of urban
streets, etc.) which influence the demand -- and hence an
overestimate of the price elasticity for this fuel. Much
of the difference between European and U.S. energy consumption is related to transportation demands. It is exceedingly
difficult to determine whether these differences are attributable to prices or to population densities and other
country-specific factors. This means that even 0.3 may be
an overestimate of σ .

In this area, the empirical evidence is by no means
clearcut. It is therefore worth reiterating the caveats
expressed in an earlier paper:

> . . . we have learned a great deal about the
> structure of energy demand within and across
> different countries. These results can be
> used to sharpen forecasts and to complement
> energy supply models, but they are plagued
> by unsolved problems, problematical data,
> and uncertain estimates. Perhaps in the end
> we will find that the limits to knowledge
> about the future are greater than the limits
> to growth in the future.
> Nordhaus (1975, p. 579)

150 Alan S. Manne

4. Concluding comments

In the area of energy policy, there are no simple answers. Given the uncertainties, it is not prudent to suppose that we can rely solely upon "soft" options such as conservation and direct solar heating. In my view, we also need coal and nuclear energy. None of these options can be neglected.

To date, despite considerable lip service to conservation and to energy independence, the net result of our political process has been that Middle Eastern oil deposits are becoming ever more vital to the U.S. economy. We and the other oil-importing nations have begun to pay for this resource by exporting weapons to all sides within the region. Oil imports are truly risky. They could lead to periodic embargoes and to nuclear confrontations that would be far more serious than the hazards of civilian nuclear energy or of coal. Our country must weigh these risks against those of imported oil. We can no longer indulge in the luxury of piecemeal decisionmaking.

References

Griffin, J. M., "An International Analysis of Demand Elasticities Between Fuel Types", final report to the National Science Foundation, RANN Division, 1977.

Hogan, W., and A. Manne, "Energy-Economy Interactions: the Fable of the Elephant and the Rabbit?", in C. J. Hitch (ed.), Modeling Energy-Economy Interactions: Five Approaches, Resources for the Future, Washington, D. C., 1977.

Modeling Resource Group, Committee on Nuclear and Alternative Energy Systems (CONAES), "Energy Modeling for an Uncertain Future", National Research Council, Washington, D. C., 1977.

Nordhaus, W. D., "The Demand for Energy: An International Perspective", in W. D. Nordhaus (ed.), Proceedings of the Workshop on Energy Demand, International Institute for Applied Systems Analysis, Laxenburg, Austria, May 1975.

7

Adjusting Capital Stock to Higher Energy-Using Efficiencies

Roger W. Sant

Background

The issue of how much energy is required for a given level of economic activity has generated considerable controversy in recent years. My own view is that this debate has been enjoyable but inconclusive, like a religious argument. The data are simply not available to answer this question.

We can intuit that the functions provided by energy, such as heat, light, and mechanical motion, are closely variable with economic activity. Since the energy required to provide those functions is determined by equipment and system efficiencies and since we know from practical experience that these efficiencies can be improved, the relationship of energy use and economic activity is nonlinear and may be discontinuous. In order to determine the exact nature of this relationship, we must ascertain precisely how the cost and other attributes of improving efficiency compare with those same factors when we produce new energy.

Unfortunately, history offers very little to enlighten us in this area. For over two decades prior to 1970, energy prices in the United States consistently declined relative to other goods in the economy. From 1950 to 1970, for example, wholesale energy prices in the aggregate dropped at the real rate of 1.7 percent per year as more energy was produced each year. As a result, the average efficiency of fuel-using capital stock

FIGURE I

Average Price and Replacement Cost of Oil and Other
Existing Energy Sources from 1950 to Mid-1976.

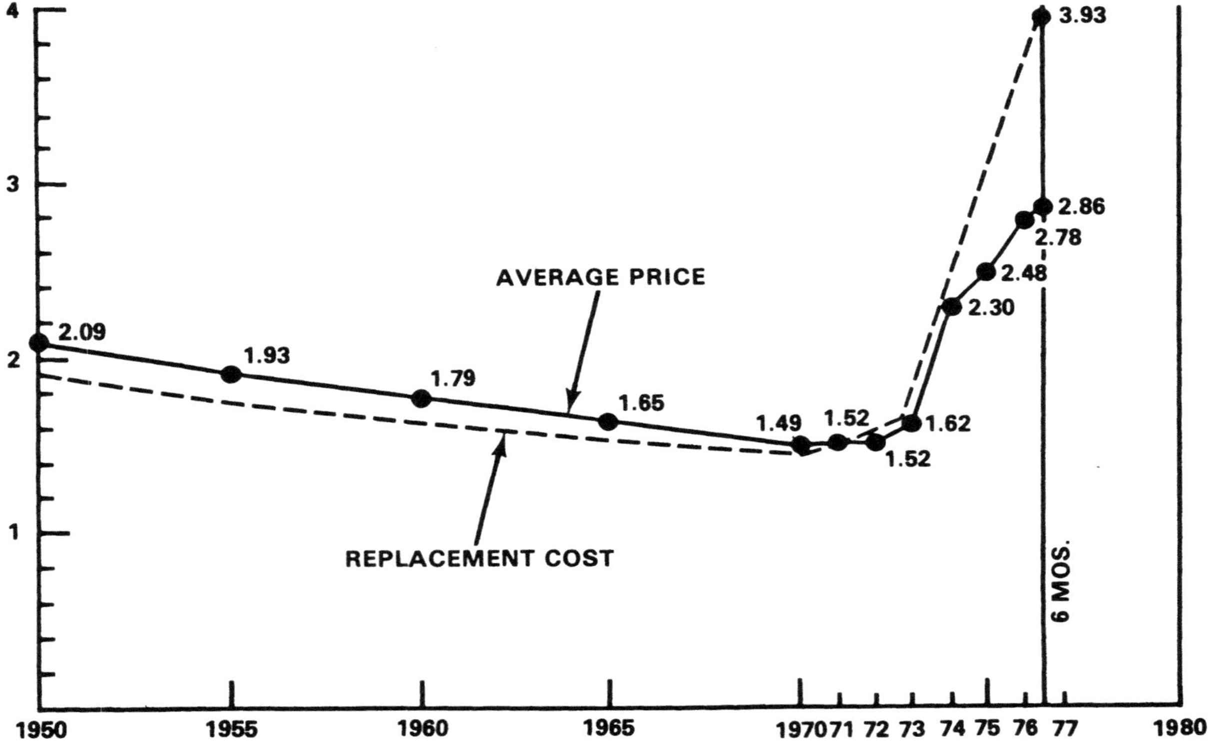

stayed relatively static throughout these years.*
There was no economic incentive for it to be
otherwise. Energy consumed was closely related
to economic conditions, viz., the gross national
product, disposable income and population growth.
Under these highly stable conditions, simple
extrapolations of energy demand worked quite well,
and econometric techniques added more precision.

However, beginning with the 1970's, the world
commenced what now appears to be a long-term
transition to higher energy prices. The Arab
oil embargo of 1973 accelerated this trend and
provided a dramatic event on which to focus public
attention. Now the average cost of replacing OPEC
oil and other existing energy sources has increased to almost 40 percent above that of the
average price paid by users as the availability
of cheaper sources declines and we can no longer
increase the size and efficiency of power plants.
This is reflected in Figure 1. Table 1 shows that
the largest disparity between present prices and
replacement costs exists with natural gas (59
percent), whereas coal is selling at about its
replacement cost. The difference for gas would be
closer to 100 percent if LNG, synthetic, or
Alaskan gas were used as the replacement fuel.

Although OPEC-related price increases were
startling, the costs of the more plentiful and
renewable sources of energy now appear to be even
higher. With these fundamental changes in energy
economics, the relative attractiveness of technical approaches to reducing demand -- more
fuel-efficient methods of providing heat, mechanical motion, and light -- has greatly increased.
Changes in the capital stock of energy-using
devices represent what might be called the
"supply" component of energy demand, e.g., increased insulation, high efficiency electric
motors, heat exchangers, lighter materials in
manufacturing automobiles, co-generation, thermal
energy storage, etc. These all have characteris-

---

*Although the efficiency of industrial energy use
improved steadily during this period it was essentially offset by declines in the residential-
commercial and transportation sectors.

TABLE I

AVERAGE PRICE AND REPLACEMENT COST OF ENERGY USED IN INDUSTRY

ENERGY FORM	PERCENT OF INDUSTRIAL USE (1977-JUNE)[1]	($ PER MILLION BTU OF DELIVERED ENERGY)		RATIO OF REPLACEMENT COST TO AVERAGE COST
		AVERAGE SPOT PRICE[2]	REPLACEMENT COST[3]	
COAL	19.0%	$1.05	$1.05[2]	1.00
PETROLEUM	34.0%	2.41	2.88[1]	1.20
NATURAL GAS	34.5%	2.08	3.30[1]	1.59
ELECTRICITY	12.5%	9.00	12.90[4]	1.43
WEIGHTED AVERAGE		$2.86	$3.93	1.37

[1] MONTHLY ENERGY REVIEW, U.S. DEPARTMENT OF ENERGY, NOVEMBER 1977.

[2] ENERGY, NOVEMBER 4, 1977, PG. 2.

[3] COST OF NEW ENERGY IF INVESTMENT MADE TODAY.

[4] CHARLES L. RUDASILL, "COMPARING COAL AND NUCLEAR COSTS", EPRI JOURNAL, OCTOBER, 1977, PG. 14.

tics that are similar to new sources of energy, in that a given investment produces a given quantity of energy; in these cases, energy is saved rather than produced. However, the potential of this new energy source has not been rigorously analyzed, particularly with regard to existing capital stock.

Of course, that portion of energy demand representing decisions to reduce usage by giving up benefits is also changed by higher energy prices. Econometric techniques may be more useful for this component; however, they have not provided generally accepted forecasts to date. This is primarily due to the fact that elasticity coefficients must be derived from data obtained during a long period of gradually declining prices.

The need to collect more reliable information on energy demand is beginning to become widely recognized. Broad national and world-wide issues of growth, stability, and world tensions hinge on a better understanding of demand-reduction opportunities.

Several analysts have begun to study the specifics of energy use. [1] In the auto sector, where relatively short product life cycles prevail, reliable data about vehicle efficiency have been collected at several institutions, [2] but little information exists about how vehicles are used. In the residential and commercial building sectors, where very long life cycles predominate, some progress has been made for new structures; however, reliable information relevant to the potential for making adjustments to existing buildings is scarce. [3] Perhaps more importantly, little is known about the degree to which home owners take action when presented with appropriate improvement opportunities. In the industrial sector, the Hatsopoulos work may be the most comprehensive to date. [4] However, the authors of that paper are the first to admit its inadequacies.

Thus, even though some recent progress has been made, the analytical tools now in existence do not measure up to the critical task of projecting credible energy demand estimates.

158   Roger W. Sant

A General Approach to the Energy Demand Forecast Problem

In recent months we have begun seeking a way to overcome these data and analytical defects. In doing so, it seems fundamental that we explicitly recognize the "supply side" of the energy demand and differentiate it from decisions to conserve by giving up energy benefits. This analysis would require the development of new baseline data on existing capital stock and energy flows within that structure. It would also be necessary to characterize each energy-saving technology to determine its cost, availability, applicability, and reliability. Given those two kinds of information, an integrating tool could be developed that would relate the cost of technically feasible physical changes that can be made in the capital stock to the cost of other energy supply technologies. Distinction would have to be made between those changes applicable to the existing capital stock (retrofit) and new additions to the stock. Also, the inherent raw material, manufacturing, and delivery system constraints on the rate of change must be taken into account.

The "supply" component of energy demand could then be coupled to a new "demand" analysis. In each of the consuming sectors, the behavioral criteria that affect energy usage and investment decisions must be researched and translated into technology adoption curves. Legal and regulatory limitations affecting decisions must also be recognized explicitly.

Even if a consensus could be reached about an appropriate substitution elasticity co-efficient, present econometric formulations would be inadequate to address these issues. As the members of the Energy Modeling Forum have said, "the aggregate substitution parameter does not provide a description of the new processes and technologies that must be developed."[5]

The Residential Sector

The specific approach suggested translates into several requirements in the residential sector:
1) A detailed engineering evaluation of a

Capital Stock and Higher Energy Efficiencies 159

statistically adequate sample of existing residences must be made. This analysis would require a complete survey of the building shell, the heating, ventilating, and air conditioning system, and the operating practices of the household. Rosenfeld has shown the feasibility of this approach in his work with California residences.[6]

2) A characterization of relevant and commercially available technologies and those that are expected to be available within the next ten years. This would allow each technology to be matched against the sample of the housing stock above.

3) An explicit test of the attractiveness of each of those technologies for the household decision-makers in each of the sample residences. This research, added to data from several focus group interviews, would allow an instrument to be prepared for surveying additional households, including renters.

4) An expansion of Hirst's work to integrate and extrapolate these data by region to the national residential sector.[7]

The Industrial Sector

In the industrial sector, the work done by Energy and Environmental Analysis, Inc. (EEA) for the Energy Research and Development Agency's (ERDA) Office of Industrial Conservation Programs as an input to the Market Oriented Program Planning Study (MOPPS) should be expanded.[8] The approach taken by EEA established a comprehensive system for comparing common energy functions in different industries (steam raising, electric drive, low temperature heating, etc.); its approach also develops consistent methods for relating industrial investments in energy conserving technologies still in the research and development stage with other means of supplying energy.

A number of steps are required to improve the flexibility, usefulness, and accuracy of this work:

1) The quality of the existing industrial

energy consumption data base must be improved. This would involve updating the data to 1975, and gathering primary data on energy using equipment by visiting the plants of a large sample of industrial users. The information required includes:

- --size and distribution of energy using equipment (e.g., electric motors, boilers, furnaces, ovens, kilns, etc.);

- --load factors;

- --thermal efficiencies;

- --age profiles;

- --specific output data (pounds of steam, temperatures, etc.);

- --Characterization of waste energy streams, by temperature range, volume, and the nature of the energy carrier, where appropriate.

This information would bring two major improvements to the EEA system. First, the aggregated base level efficiencies (currently estimated industry by industry and function by function) could be validated and modified where necessary. An accurate gauge of the distribution of the current efficiencies is critical for sensible policy and program decisions. Second, the functions/services sector used in MOPPS could be further disaggregated where appropriate. The "machine drive" function, for example, is provided by both electrically and mechanically power engines. The National Academy of Sciences study, "Energy Consumption Measurement: Data Needs for Public Policy," suggested these same steps.

2) The potential efficiencies and related costs of currently available energy conservation technologies for both new plants and retrofit applications needs to be characterized and added to the MOPPS model. This would allow these technologies to compete analytically with both new energy

Capital Stock and Higher Energy Efficiencies   161

sources and developing technologies. The
result would be a precise specification of
what technologies are responsible for base
case results of industrial energy use that
are different from the projected growth rate
in industrial output.

3) The decision-making behavior and innova-
tive technologies penetration rates in the
MOPPS model must be explicitly derived from
primary data. As it exists, the model re-
lies on econometric estimates for market
penetration rates, and has an invariant
retirement rate for the existing capital
stock. Specific market research should allow
a better understanding of the sets of decisions that determine the penetration curves
by quantifying the primary factors.

4) The data work in step one could then be
integrated into the existing Department of
Energy energy-use data base and incorporated
in the industrial portion of the MOPPS model.

The Commercial Building and Transportation Sectors

The approach for both the commercial and
transportation sectors would follow paths similar
to the work in the residential and industrial
sectors. Accordingly, the details need not be
spelled out again. However, it is expected that
the analysis in these sectors could draw heavily
on work already begun at several institutions.

The Integrating Tool

There is need for each of these sector
models to be capable of stand-alone operation,
given exogenous specifications of key variables
(e.g., energy prices, determinants of levels of
service desired, etc.). As noted, each sector
model could be sufficiently disaggregated to
permit detailed study of alternative technologies
in terms of processes, geography, weather, etc.
Each model, thus, would be capable of producing
results that could become inputs to more aggregate energy sector models.

Initially, the highest level of aggregation
ought to be an integrating model. Its main

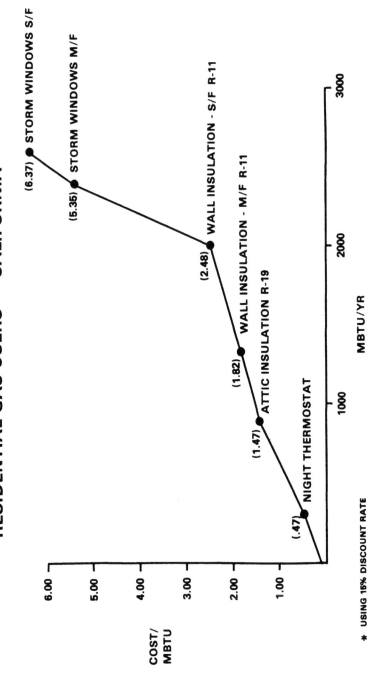

purpose would be to integrate the independent results of the more disaggregated, subsidiary models. This would make it possible to evaluate the trade-offs between conventional energy supply and the energy conserving technologies utilized from points of extraction to points where energy changes form into work.

The model should be initially oriented toward the next ten years with results through the year 2000. Its format should be of a sectoral equilibrium nature. The model itself ultimately could be linked to or included in a comprehensive general equilibrium growth model or a comprehensive energy sector model with a rich structure.

Preliminary Results

Some of the research and analysis called for in this paper has been completed at various institutions. Although this work is far from adequate, it can be used to illustrate the kind of information that would be available if the overall task were completed. It also establishes some patterns and justifies certain preliminary conclusions:

1) The supply of "conservation energy" can be characterized so that it can be compared directly with conventional energy supplies. For instance, Figure 2 describes Rosenfeld's findings in the residential gas market of California in traditional supply curve terms. As shown, some of the conserving technologies are currently competitive with gas supplies and some are not. For example, storm windows in multi-family dwellings require $5.35 per mcf gas in order to be competitive, whereas the current residential price is approximately $3.00. If apartment dwellers in California were paying directly for Alaskan gas, their price would be much closer to $5.35 and storm windows would become competitive technologies. Storm windows on single family residences would probably be cheaper than converting to electric heat.

2) Hirst indicates that if current replacement cost prices are used, a total of $40 billion in improvements to residential

Table 2
Composite of Preliminary Findings:
The Major Technologies

SECTOR *	CAPITAL COSTS 1978 - 1985 (IN $10⁹ OF 1977 DOLLARS)	TOTAL COST/ $10⁶ BTU SAVED	TOTAL ENERGY SAVED (IN QUADS) IN 1985
AUTOMOBILES	5.8	1.02*	2.0
RESIDENTIAL	40.0	2.86*	2.4
INDUSTRIAL	126.0	2.70	10.0
COMMERCIAL	45.8	1.42*	5.5
TOTAL	217.6	2.19	19.9

* AUTHOR'S ESTIMATES USING 15% DISCOUNT RATE; 5 YEARS FOR AUTOMOBILES, 15 YEARS FOR RESIDENTIAL AND COMMERCIAL BUILDINGS.

* SOURCE: FOOTNOTES 14, 13, 4, 15

capital stock would be competitive, saving
2.4 quads in 1985. This analysis, although
needing further refinement, indicates a
rough approximation of capital investment
that is competitive and the energy saving
that would be produced.

3) The preliminary work by Hatsopoulos et
al cited earlier indicates that an investment of $126 billion, resulting in savings
of approximately 10.0 quads of industrial
energy in 1985, is competitive at marginal
cost prices of energy.

4) The Federal Task Force On Motor Vehicles
Goals Beyond 1980 indicates that to meet
the mandated standard of 27.5 miles per
gallon by 1985, an additional investment by
the auto industry of $5.8 billion would
be required. This investment would produce
approximately two quads of energy by 1985.[10]

5) Dr. Jerry Jackson at Oak Ridge Labora-
tories has made a preliminary analysis with
his commercial building model. The results
suggest that a $45.8 billion investment,
saving 5.5 quads in 1985, is competitive with
marginal cost prices. [11]

A composite of these preliminary findings
is shown in Table II. This table only represents
the major technologies; it does not include the
hundreds of less significant but still important
technologies that should be considered. At the
same time, it must again be pointed out that there
are obvious holes in the data used. The findings
primarily illustrate the approach proposed and
give a rough approximation of the level of investment justified at the margin to achieve higher
energy using efficiencies. These figures include
technologies for new construction and incorporate
improvements in the automobile and appliance stock
that could take place by 1985. New industrial
process technologies are not included in these
results. These preliminary assessments also do
not reflect the effects of decision-making behavior. Because so little of the behavioral data
has been collected, one can only surmise that the
amount of investment and savings actually occur-
ring would be substantially less than the

166   *Roger W. Sant*

potential shown.

These preliminary data, in addition to evoking questions about their accuracy, raise the question of how much conservation there is above the marginal cost point. Clearly, the slope of the conservation supply curve going through the marginal cost point and beyond has great significance. The approach suggested would provide this information.

Conclusion

It is suggested in this paper that additional data collection and analysis is needed to substantially overcome the defects of present energy demand forecasting techniques. The technical potential for conservation must be veridically defined and the difference between the potential and likely results from consumer decisions must be carefully assessed.

Existing data have shown the validity of the approach suggested and have provided very rough estimates about the potential. Nevertheless, it is contended that until a more complete assessment is made, it will be difficult to understand the relationship of energy use and economic activity. It will be even more difficult to assess policies designed to reduce energy use.

REFERENCES

(1) A good example is M.H. Ross and R.H. Williams, "The Potential for Fuel Conservation," Technology Review, February 1977.

(2) The report by the Federal Task Force on "Motor Vehicles Goals Beyond 1980," September 2, 1977, summarizes these results.

(3) The most comprehensive project in the residential area is E. Hirst and V. Carney, "Residential Energy Use to the Year 2000," Oak Ridge National Laboratory, September, 1977. Oak Ridge National Laboratory is about to publish similar information for commercial buildings.

(4) G. Hatsopoulos, E. Gyftopoulos, R. Sant, and T. Widmer, "Capital Investment for Industrial

Capital Stock and Higher Energy Efficiencies 167

Energy Efficiency," Harvard Business Review, March-April, 1978 (to be published).

(5) Energy Modeling Forum, "Energy and the Economy," EMF Report I, Volume I, September, 1977, p. 15.

(6) A.H. Rosenfeld, "Some Potentials for Energy and Peak Power Conservation in California," Department of Physics and Lawrence Berkeley Laboratory, University of California at Berkeley (to appear in the Proceedings of the International Conference on Energy Use Management, Tuscon, Arizona, October 1977, Pergamon Press).

(7) E. Hirst, et al, "An Improved Engineering-Economic Model of Residential Energy Use," Oak Ridge National Labs, April, 1977.

(8) Industrial Sector Working Group, Market Oriented Program Planning Study (MOPPS), final report review draft, September 30, 1977.

(9) E. Hirst and J. Carney, "Residential Energy Use to the Year 2000: Conservation and Economics," Oak Ridge National Labs, September, 1977.

(10) Report by the Federal Task Force on Motor Vehicle Goals Beyond 1980, Volume 2, September 2, 1976.

(11) Private conversation with J.R. Jackson, based on preliminary analysis, Oak Ridge National Labs, January 18, 1978.